Henry V

Henry V

by William Shakespeare

A screen adaptation by Kenneth Branagh

Chatto & Windus

LONDON

Published in 1989 by
Chatto & Windus Ltd
30 Bedford Square
London WC1B 3SG

A CIP Catalogue record for this book is available from the British Library

ISBN 0 7011 3536 0

The original soundtrack recording, with Patrick Doyle's score played by the City of Birmingham Symphony Orchestra under Simon Rattle, is available from EMI on CD and cassette (CDC 7 49919 2/EL 7 49919 4).

Design Shawn Webb

Set and printed by Butler & Tanner Ltd, Frome and London

Acknowledgements

Thanks are due to all the actors and members
of the production team who suggested useful
changes to the screenplay as we went along
especially our technical advisers, Professor
Russell Jackson and Hugh Cruttwell who were
particularly helpful. Thanks also to Adrian
Noble whose magnificent RSC production of
Henry V was an inspiration to this film version.
Finally, thanks to Annie Wotton who recorded
every twist and turn in the screenplay's
development with her customary excellence.
Thank you all.

For Stephen Evans

who made it all possible

Chorus	DEREK JACOBI	Costume Designer
Henry V	KENNETH BRANAGH	**PHYLLIS DALTON**
Gloucester	SIMON SHEPHERD	
Bedford	JAMES LARKIN	
Exeter	BRIAN BLESSED	Production Designer
York	JAMES SIMMONS	**TIM HARVEY**
Westmoreland	PAUL GREGORY	
Canterbury	CHARLES KAY	
Ely	ALEC McCOWEN	Editor
Cambridge	FABIAN CARTWRIGHT	**MICHAEL BRADSELL**
Scroop	STEPHEN SIMMS	
Grey	JAY VILLIERS	
Erpingham	EDWARD JEWESBURY	Director of Photography
Fluellen	IAN HOLM	**KENNETH MacMILLAN B.S.C.**
Gower	DANIEL WEBB	
Jamy	JIMMY YUILL	
Macmorris	JOHN SESSIONS	Associate Producer
Bates	SHAUN PRENDERGAST	**DAVID PARFITT**
Court	PAT DOYLE	
Williams	MICHAEL WILLIAMS	
Bardolph	RICHARD BRIERS	Music Composed by
Nym	GEOFFREY HUTCHINGS	**PATRICK DOYLE**
Pistol	ROBERT STEPHENS	
Falstaff	ROBBIE COLTRANE	
Boy	CHRISTIAN BALE	Music Performed by
Mistress Quickly	JUDI DENCH	**CITY OF BIRMINGHAM**
French King	PAUL SCOFIELD	**SYMPHONY ORCHESTRA**
Dauphin	MICHAEL MALONEY	
Burgundy	HAROLD INNOCENT	
Orleans	RICHARD CLIFFORD	
Grandpré	COLIN HURLEY	Conducted by
Constable	RICHARD EASTON	**SIMON RATTLE**
Mountjoy	CHRISTOPHER RAVENSCROFT	
Katherine	EMMA THOMPSON	Executive Producer
Alice	GERALDINE McEWAN	**STEPHEN EVANS**
Governor of Harfleur	DAVID LLOYD MEREDITH	
Messenger	DAVID PARFITT	
Warwick	NICHOLAS FERGUSON	Produced by
Talbot	TOM WHITEHOUSE	**BRUCE SHARMAN**
Berri	NIGEL GREAVES	
Bretagne	JULIAN GARTSIDE	
1st Soldier	MARK INMAN	Directed by
2nd Soldier	CHRIS ARMSTRONG	**KENNETH BRANAGH**
Child	CALUM YUILL	

Introduction

I first became seriously interested in *Henry V* when I was training to be an actor. Constantly on the look-out for unusual Shakespearean audition speeches, I scoured the famous text for something that wasn't just 'full of quotes'. Like many students I knew 'Once more unto the breach' and the St Crispin's Day speech, but I was very surprised at how unfamiliar this most popular of plays seemed. I discovered the king's marvellous tirade against Scroop as well as his terrifying speech to the governor of Harfleur, but apart from these meaty passages for the young actor, the play itself was a constant surprise. For a modern audience, the abiding image of *Henry V* is provided by Sir Laurence Olivier's famous film version, but the powerful Elizabethan pageantry and chivalric splendour of that extraordinary movie did not accord with the impression I received as I read the text afresh. To me, the play seemed darker, harsher, and the language more bloody and muscular than I remembered. Although I was aware of bringing a particular set of post-war sensibilities to bear on my reading, I sensed that a 1980s film version of such a piece would make for a profoundly different experience.

In 1984, I played Henry V for the Royal Shakespeare Company in a production by the brilliant young director, Adrian Noble, which confirmed for me the marvellous potential for modern views of the play. Although Olivier's film had been welcomed and celebrated as part of the war effort, its seeming nationalistic and militaristic emphasis had created a great deal of suspicion and doubt about the value of *Henry V* for a late twentieth-century audience. The play is performed very rarely and the RSC production was their first for ten years. Although understandable in some ways, this apparent lack of confidence struck me as unfair. It is a more complex play than is traditionally acknowledged and Adrian's production strongly resisted the concept of a two-dimensional *Boy's Own* adventure. In my own performance, I tried to realise the qualities of introspection, fear, doubt and anger which I believed the text indicated: an especially young Henry with more than a little of the Hamlet in him. It was conveying these elements of the king's personality that gave me the initial idea for a new screen version – the idea of abandoning large-theatre projection and allowing close-ups and low-level dialogue to draw the audience deep into the human side of this distant medieval world. I thought that the combination of this concentration with the strong visual possibilities of the siege of Harfleur and the battle of Agincourt might produce an extraordinary modern film. And when I left the RSC in 1985, after playing the part for nearly two years, I was already producing a mental 'storyboard' for the movie version.

In 1987, Stephen Evans joined the Renaissance Theatre Company, which I had recently formed with David Parfitt. Stephen became our executive director, with special responsibility for the financial structure of the company and, apart from an eighteen-month programme of touring Shakespeare, I immediately told Stephen of my other plans – in particular, a film of *Henry V*. By now, I had decided that not only did I want to adapt the play for the screen, but I wanted to direct it as well. I sold him the concept as enthusiastically as I could – my (unsurprising) view of the play as being tremendously 'filmic', with an exciting linear plot, short scenes, great structural variety and several different strains of narrative providing a rich mixture of low-life sleaze, foreign sophistication, romance, action, philosophy and humour. In all seriousness, I was convinced that I could make a truly popular film: there would be no declamatory acting and the pace and excitement of the plot would be presented with the greatest possible clarity and immediacy. It was a story that would make you laugh, make you cry, and be utterly accessible to anyone of whatever age and background. These were all ingredients that would be needed to persuade Stephen's financial contacts to invest in the film.

I was relentlessly enthusiastic, and Stephen took me at my word. If what I said was true, then he could raise the money for the film, but first he needed the screenplay, which would have to reflect the imaginative approach I had described. If, as I claimed, *Henry V* could work as a political thriller, as a detailed analysis of leadership and a complex debate about war – and that was just for starters – then this would have to be made clear from the outset. A great deal of description would be necessary to illustrate our approach, and to allow the sometimes sterile world of film finance to

Think, when we talk of horses, that you see them
Printing their proud hoofs in the receiving earth.

I started work on the first draft in January 1988. It seemed clear that a great deal of the text would have to be cut, as I was determined that the film should be of a commercial length, which I estimated at two hours. In the theatre, the last RSC production played for over three hours, even with significant cuts, and there was no choice but to be even more savage. My own experience of cinema-going convinced me that two hours was the maximum span of concentration that could be expected from an audience for a film of this kind. In any case, the cuts dictated themselves. The more tortuous aspects of the Fluellen/Pistol antagonism, culminating in the resoundingly unfunny leek scene, were the first to go. The double-edged exchanges between Henry and Burgundy in Act V also, for my purposes, failed to advance the plot, and added little to the aspects of the play that we wanted to explore. Elsewhere, there were trimmings of Elizabethan obscurities, particularly in the language of the Boar's Head scenes, with only the most delicious-sounding phrases escaping sacrifice on the altar of instant under-standing. Plot repetitions and excessive flights of rhetorical fancy were ruthlessly excised.

Once into shooting, further trimming would be suggested by actors (who also asked for some restorations) and yet more trim-ming was done in the editing process. I wanted there to be no fat on the film at all, and I was certain that the actors we had cast would seize this opportunity for economy. Many of them had been in the play before, some in the same roles. For the others, there was the cut text to draw on as their 'subtext'. Everyone in the cast rose to the challenge supremely well and made the language sound utterly real without denying the poetry and magical prose that gave the film a special dimension of its own.

There were other practical problems to face. In the opening speech, the Chorus refers to Shakespeare's own theatre. I wanted to place our Chorus in a disused theatre, and have the character deliver the speech while walking through an empty auditorium, eventually throwing open scenery doors to allow the camera to travel outside and into the 'real' world of our film. Early script discussions suggested the idea of starting in an empty film studio, and since much of the opening scene can be interpreted as alluding to the mystery and imagination employed in the medium of film, it seemed the proper and honest way to start. After that, much of the Chorus's contribution was broken up, with some speeches in voice-over, to aid clarity and to maximise the eery effect of his presence.

I decided on including some significant scenes that Olivier's film, for obvious reasons, had left out: in particular, the conspirators' scene where Henry stage-manages a public cashiering of the bosom friends who have been revealed as traitors. The violence and extremism of Henry's behaviour and its effect on a volatile war cabinet were elements that the Olivier version was not likely to spotlight. I reinstated the savage threat to the Governor of Harfleur where the king talks of possible rape and infanticide, a speech which underlines the crueller aspects of an increasingly desperate English military campaign.

I also decided to go one step further in bringing the character of Falstaff firmly into the action. It was important for an audience that might have no previous knowledge of the *Henry IV* plays to have an idea of the background to *Henry V*, and I wanted to achieve the greatest possible impact from Mistress Quickly's speech reporting the death of Falstaff, a character that the audience would not otherwise have encountered.

I constructed this brief flashback from three separate scenes in the *Henry IV* plays. My intention was to give, in miniature, a sense of Falstaff's place among the surviving members of the Boar's Head crew, and to make clear his former relationship and estrangement from the young monarch. Both this scene and the flashback during Bardolph's on-screen execution help to illustrate the young king's intense isolation and his difficulty in rejecting his former tavern life.

There were also minor changes. Occasionally I used short words and phrases from elsewhere in the play to allow certain truncated sections to 'scan', usually so that a line of verse could be completed. These are all liberties of a sort, but I hope they are Shakespearean in spirit – as I hope we have remained true to the spirit of the play. Above all the aim of the screenplay has been to bring out what some critics have referred to as 'the play within the play': an uncompromising view of politics and a deeply questioning, ever-relevant and compassionate survey of people and war.

Film Studio: day

Darkness. A match is struck. It illuminates the face of the **Chorus**. The manner is conversational, friendly, intimate. He welcomes us with the clarity and warmth of the great story-teller. As he starts to speak, the camera slowly moves away from him.

> CHORUS
> O, for a muse of fire, that would ascend
> The brightest heaven of invention.

The match remains alight as he moves down a metal staircase, the camera following him as he stops beside an enormous light switch. He pulls the switch, activating the lights around him. He discards the match and moves on.

CHORUS
A kingdom for a stage, princes to act
And monarchs to behold the swelling scene!
Then should the warlike Harry, like himself,
Assume the port of Mars; and at his heels,
Leash'd in like hounds, should famine, sword and fire
Crouch for employment. But pardon gentles all.

It is clear that we are in a deserted film studio. The **Chorus** stands on a low platform in the centre of the stage, surveying the scene. A few lamps are alight behind him, a camera, odd props and half-painted scenery are scattered about.

CHORUS
The flat unraised spirits that have dared
On this unworthy scaffold to bring forth
So great an object:

He moves on, passing pieces of set marked H.V. He speaks to camera like some mysterious MC.

CHORUS
Can this cockpit hold
The vasty fields of France? or may we cram
Within this wooden O the very casques
That did affright the air at Agincourt?
O, pardon!
And let us ciphers to this great account
On your imaginary forces work.
For 'tis your thoughts that now must deck our kings
Carry them here and there, jumping o'er times,
Turning the accomplishment of many years
Into an hour-glass:

The **Chorus** now starts to lead us towards huge wooden doors in a semi-constructed set.

CHORUS
For the which supply,
Admit me Chorus to this history;
Who prologue-like your humble patience pray,
Gently to hear, kindly to judge, our ...
... Play!

With a dramatic flourish he turns to fling open the doors revealing an ominous **Darkness.**

Corridor of Henry's Palace: night

We hear the latch of a door and see a narrow strip of light. A door is opened. A sinister silhouette appears in the room beyond.

Candlelit Chamber: night

It is **Canterbury** standing at the door, nervously checking the corridor outside.

CANTERBURY
My lord, I'll tell you:

He quietly closes the door and moves into the small darkened room to sit opposite **Ely**. They are urgently discussing the implications of a new anti-church bill and how best to avoid it by involving the King. They are seasoned, worried politicians on their mettle. Born survivors, now time is against them. The course of action is clear. They will be ruthless in urging the King to France, where matters spiritual will be forgotten. The atmosphere is tense and conspiratorial.

CANTERBURY
That self bill is urg'd
Which in the eleventh year of the last king's reign
Was like to have passed against us.
ELY
But how, my lord, shall we resist it now?
CANTERBURY
It must be thought on. If it pass against us,
We lose the better half of our possession:
ELY
But what prevention?
CANTERBURY
The king is full of grace and fair regard.
ELY
And a true lover of the holy church.
CANTERBURY
The courses of his youth promised it not.
Since his addiction was to courses vain;
His hours filled up with riots, banquets, sports;
And never noted in him any study.
ELY
But, my good lord,
How now for mitigation of this bill
Urged by the commons? Doth his majesty
Incline to it, or no?

CANTERBURY
He seems indifferent,
Or rather swaying more upon our part
For I have made an offer to his majesty
As touching France ...

Before **Canterbury** can reveal the nature of this offer they hear the sound of footsteps outside the door and hurry to see ...

Corridor, Henry's Palace: night

The shadow of a cloaked figure surrounded by four guards moves impressively along the palace wall.

Council Chamber, Henry's Palace: night

The great doors of the Council Chamber open to reveal the English nobles already gathered in a smoky torch-lit atmosphere of expectation. They turn to look, and see the mysterious silhouette of a cloaked figure in the doorway. As the figure starts to move into the room, the nobles take up their places in the Chamber, which resembles a medieval house of commons.

We do not see the face as the **Camera tracks** behind the cloaked figure, passing the expectant looks of his assembled Council, who bow as he makes the long walk to the throne.

Each political faction of England is there. The King's brothers, **Gloucester** and **Bedford,** his uncle **Exeter,** his cousin **York,** his nobles and generals, **Erpingham, Westmoreland, Scroop, Grey** and **Cambridge,** soon to be joined by the church. It's like a meeting of Mafia chiefs with the young King uneasily in charge but betraying little of his nervousness. The army of vested interests hungry for conquest, money and blood look ready to turn on the King himself if this Council fails to produce the 'right' decision on France.

The Council sits.

At last we see the young monarch's face. He is twenty-seven years old and the leader of the most volatile and powerful country in the medieval world. This solitary, pensive boy in 'the very May morn of his youth' is **King Henry V** of England.

> HENRY V
> Where is my gracious lord of Canterbury?

At which point the breathless clerics, **Canterbury** and **Ely,** enter the Chamber and make their way towards the throne, to kneel before him.

> CANTERBURY
> God and his angels guard your sacred throne
> And make you long become it!
> HENRY V
> Sure, we thank you.
> My learned lord, we pray you to proceed,
> And justly and religiously unfold
> Why the law Salic that they have in France
> Or should, or should not, bar us in our claim.

As **Canterbury** starts to rise, **Henry** continues in a tone of warning, surprising the clerics and his nobles.

> HENRY V
> And pray take heed how you impawn our person,
> How you awake our sleeping sword of war:
> We charge you in the name of God take heed;
> For never two such kingdoms did contend
> Without much fall of blood;

Exeter and **Westmoreland** exchange looks with the chastened clerics. The decision on France will not be achieved as easily as they had hoped.

CANTERBURY
Then hear me gracious sovereign,
There is no bar
To make against your highness' claim to France
But this, which they produce from Pharamond,
In terram Salicam mulieres ne succedant,
'No woman shall succeed in Salic land';

He begins to pace the Council Chamber directing his speech to the assembled nobility as if in a court room.

CANTERBURY
Which Salic land the French unjustly gloze
To be the realm of France.
Yet their own authors faithfully affirm
That the land Salic lies in Germany
Between the floods of Sala and of Elbe;
Then doth it well appear this Salic law
Was not devised for the realm of France;
Nor did the French possess the Salic land
Until four hundred one and twenty years
After defunction of King Pharamond,
Idly supposed the founder of this law;

He slaps the document in his hand with a flourish, pausing for a moment to round on his rapt audience. He is now in his stride and takes evident relish in the absurd complexity of what is to follow. Henry and the wiser nobles know better than to dismiss this wily politician as an eccentric fool.

CANTERBURY
King Pepin which deposed Childeric,
Did as heir general, being descended
Of Blithild, which was the daughter to King Clothair,
Make claim and title to the crown of France.
Hugh Capet also, who usurped the crown
Of Charles the Duke of Lorraine, sole heir male
Of the true line and stock of Charles the Great,
Could not keep quiet in his conscience,
Wearing the crown of France, till satisfied
That fair Queen Isabel, his grandmother
Was lineal of the Lady Ermengare,
Daughter to Charles the aforesaid Duke of Lorraine:
By the which marriage the line of Charles the Great
Was reunited to the crown of France.

Canterbury pauses briefly beside **Exeter,** who throws him a threatening glance. It is time to play the only ace.

> CANTERBURY
> So that, as clear as is the summer's sun,

Uneasy laughter and nervous looks compound the conspiracy to convince the **King** at all costs.

> CANTERBURY
> All appear
> To hold in right and title of the female:
> So do the Kings of France unto this day;
> Howbeit they would hold up this Salic law
> To bar your highness claiming from the female.

Canterbury kneels before the **King.** His case is complete. Henry fixes him with an unflinching, penetrating stare. He will ask only once more.

> HENRY V
> May I with right and conscience make this claim?

The words 'right' and 'conscience' hang in the air as the Archbishop pauses, holding the monarch's gaze.

> CANTERBURY
> The sin upon my head, dread sovereign!
> Stand for your own; unwind your bloody flag;

The warlords move in to lobby. First **Exeter.** Martial Lord. A helpful friend, a terrifying enemy.

> EXETER
> Your brother kings and monarchs of the earth
> Do all expect that you should rouse yourself,
> As did the former lions of your blood.

Now **Westmoreland** less fierce and calculating than **Exeter** but just as intent.

> WESTMORELAND
> Never king of England
> Had nobles richer, and more loyal subjects,
> Whose hearts have left their bodies here in England
> And lie pavilioned in the fields of France.

Finally **Canterbury,** in for the kill. **Ely** moves towards the **King;** adding weight to the point.

> CANTERBURY
> O, let their bodies follow my dear liege,

23

With blood and sword and fire to win your right;
In aid whereof we of the spirituality
Will raise your highness such a mighty sum
As never did the clergy at one time
Bring in to any of your ancestors.

Behind unfathomable eyes the young soldier king affects to weigh interests commercial, spiritual and political attendant on the enterprise. What he genuinely feels or thinks is uncertain, but after a pause his decision seems clear.

HENRY
Call in the messengers sent from the Dauphin.

Exeter and Westmoreland, relieved that the King has made the right choice, swiftly resume their seats and wait to hear the news from France. The King quickly and uneasily takes up the public tone.

HENRY V
Now are we well resolved; and by God's help,
And yours, the noble sinews of our power,
France being ours, we'll bend it to our awe.

Then remotely, almost to himself, as he watches the large doors open,

HENRY V
Or break it all to pieces.

Montjoy, the French Herald, enters the chamber, with an attendant.

HENRY V
Now are we well prepared to know the pleasure
Of our fair cousin Dauphin.
MONTJOY
Your highness lately sending into France
Did claim some certain dukedoms, in the right
Of your great predecessor, King Edward the Third.
In answer of which claim, the prince my master
Says that you savour too much of your youth.
He therefore sends you, meeter for your spirit,
This tun of treasure;

Exeter calls the messenger to him with a curt nod.

MONTJOY
And in lieu of this,
Desires you that the dukedoms that you claim
Hear no more of you. This the Dauphin speaks.
HENRY V
What treasure, uncle?

The messenger opens the box and reveals its contents.

EXETER
Tennis-balls, my liege.

The court wait, the atmosphere even more tense. How will he
react? The **King** begins to speak quietly with threatening dignity.

HENRY V

We are glad the Dauphin is so pleasant with us;
His present and your pains we thank you for:
When we have matched our rackets to these balls,
We will in France, by God's grace, play a set
Shall strike his father's crown into the hazard.
And we understand him well
How he comes o'er us with our wilder days,
Not measuring what use we made of them.

Henry rises from the throne, the rest of the court stand. As he
moves slowly and threateningly towards the startled **Montjoy**,
Henry begins to show the potential force of his rule and his resolve
for France.

HENRY V

But tell the Dauphin I will keep my state,
Be like a king and show my sail of greatness
When I do rouse me in my throne of France.
And tell the pleasant prince this mock of his
Hath turned his balls to gun-stones; and his soul
Shall stand sore charged for the wasteful vengeance
That shall fly with them:

Henry's anger has built into an explosion of outrage undeniable
in its force. Even the court cynics are forced to consider the
genuineness of the **King's** feelings. He continues to move towards
Montjoy.

HENRY V

For many a thousand widows
Shall this his mock mock out of their dear husbands;
Mock mothers from their sons, mock castles down;
And some are yet ungotten and unborn
That shall have cause to curse the Dauphin's scorn.

His rage subsides, leaving the court momentarily unsteady.

HENRY V

So get you hence in peace; and tell the Dauphin
His jest will savour but of shallow wit
When thousands weep more than did laugh at it.

And then a remarkable change of tone and with great gentleness,
he signals to **Cambridge** and **Grey**.

HENRY V

26   Convey them with safe conduct. Fare you well.

Montjoy takes his leave, surprised and impressed, with much to tell the French court of this 'boy' King.

As they leave, **Exeter** approaches.

> EXETER
> This was a merry message.
> HENRY V
> We hope to make the sender blush at it.

Henry returns to his throne. Now for action.

> HENRY V
> Therefore, my lords, omit no happy hour,
> That may give furtherance to our expedition;
> For we have now no thought in us but France,
> Save those to God that run before our business.

He moves off, his manner urgent and determined, followed by the now united court.

> HENRY V
> Therefore let every man now task his thought
> That this fair action may on foot be brought.

As they sweep out of the Chamber, **Canterbury** and **Ely** at the back of the group turn to each other, and share a smile of dark relief.

CUT TO:

Boar's Head Tavern: day

Closed shutters are opened. Sunlight floods onto the face of an old man fighting a monstrous hangover. He turns and moves into the tavern, revealing the filth and debris of the place. We hear the voice of the **Chorus,** gently ironic.

> CHORUS
> (Voice-over)
> Now all the youth of England are on fire.
> For now sits Expectation in the air
> And hides a sword from hilts unto the point
> With crowns imperial, crowns and coronets
> Promised to Harry and his followers.

During this the camera has revealed the hunched figure of **Bardolph** moving round the tavern staircase, looking for scraps of food like some scavenging animal. He sits down at a table laden with left-overs. A cat is happily feeding. Also at the table is **Nym,** very much the worse for wear after a hard night's drinking. **Bardolph**   27 pushes the cat off the table, and tears at a piece of fowl. He launches into an annoyingly breezy greeting.

BARDOLPH
Well met, Corporal Nym.
NYM
Good morrow, Lieutenant Bardolph.

The cat gives a plaintive miaow. **Bardolph** throws a mug of stale beer at it. He is still searching for gossip.

BARDOLPH
What, are you and Ancient Pistol friends yet?

Nym shoots him a withering glance. Clearly a sensitive subject. He replies in sullen tones.

NYM
For my part, I care not; I say little;
but when time shall serve there shall be smiles;
but that shall be as it may.

He finishes on a note of mysterious triumph which even he fails to understand.

BARDOLPH
Come, I will bestow a breakfast to make you friends
and we'll be all three sworn brothers to France:
let it be so, good Corporal Nym.
NYM
I will do as I may.

Bardolph decides to change tack, and sides with his aggrieved companion. Not losing the chance to stir things up at the same time.

BARDOLPH
It is certain, corporal, that Ancient Pistol
is married to Nell Quickly; and certainly she
did you wrong, for you were betrothed to her.

At this moment the two middle-aged soldiers of misfortune are interrupted by the appearance of **Nym**'s adversary, **Pistol**, and his **Mistress Quickly**. A squeal of pleasure from **Mistress Quickly** as **Pistol** chases her lasciviously around a ladder, to be brought up short by seeing **Nym**, now standing, sword in hand, facing them. As **Mistress Quickly** wipes her filthy hands, **Nym** greets **Pistol**.

NYM
How now, mine host Pistol!

Pistol, the wayward wordsmith, takes immediate, exaggerated and indignant offence.

PISTOL
Base tike, call'st thou me host?
Now, by this hand I swear, I scorn the term;
Nor shall my Nell keep lodgers.

She picks up on the tone of colourful contempt.

MISTRESS QUICKLY
No, by my troth, not long; for we cannot
lodge or board a dozen or fourteen
gentlewomen that live honestly by the
prick of their needles, but it shall be
thought we keep a bawdy-house straight.

Nym is maddened by the pair.

NYM
Pish!
PISTOL
Pish for thee, Iceland dog!

Bardolph flinches as **Mistress Quickly** intervenes, moving towards **Nym**, filling the room with a sense of seedy bustle.

MISTRESS QUICKLY
Good Corporal Nym, show thy valour and
put up thy sword.
NYM
Will you shog off!

Mistress Quickly, alarmed by the vehemence of **Nym**'s tone, runs back up the stairs to the arms of her husband.

> NYM
> Pistol, I would prick your guts a little,
> in good terms, as I may; and that's the
> humour of it.
> PISTOL
> O braggard vile!

It is now **Bardolph's** turn to step in, drawing his sword, he puts himself between the two men.

> BARDOLPH
> Hear me, hear me what I say: he that
> strikes the first stroke, I'll run him
> up to the hilts as I am a soldier.

Pistol cheerfully seizes on this way out.

> PISTOL
> **An oath of mickle might; and fury shall abate.**

Before **Nym** has a chance to react, the **Boy** rushes down the stairs. He has come direct from the ailing **Falstaff,** most famed among this group of the King's former drinking and thieving companions, and now rejected by the young monarch.

> BOY
> Mine host Pistol, you must come to my
> master, and you hostess: he is very
> sick, and would to bed. Good Bardolph,
> put thy face between his sheets and do
> the office of a warming pan.
> BARDOLPH
> Away, you rogue!

The **Boy's** tone changes; he is deadly serious.

> BOY
> Faith, he's very ill.

As the **Boy** makes his way back up the stairs, **Mistress Quickly** is caught by the melancholy of the moment. She speaks with quiet regret.

> MISTRESS QUICKLY
> By my troth, the King has killed his heart.
> Good husband, come in presently.

She follows the **Boy** up towards the bedroom which **Falstaff** has now occupied.

Falstaff's Bedroom, Boar's Head: day

In close-up the face of the dying **Falstaff,** his eyes closed, not moving. **Mistress Quickly** leans over him, searching for some sign of hope, knowing it will be over soon.

Boar's Head Tavern: day

Nym, Bardolph and **Pistol** gathered together, looking up towards the room where their sick and abandoned friend lies. The atmosphere has changed, but still the two braggarts resist **Bardolph**'s conciliation.

> BARDOLPH
> Come, shall I make you two friends?
> We must to France together. Why the
> devil should we keep knives to cut
> one another's throats?
> NYM
> You'll pay me the eight shillings I
> won of you at betting?
> PISTOL
> Base is the slave that pays.

As **Nym** starts to draw his sword again, **Bardolph** intervenes.

> BARDOLPH
> By this sword, he that makes the first
> thrust, I'll kill him; by this sword
> I will.

Mistress Quickly returns to interrupt this exchange.

> MISTRESS QUICKLY
> As ever you come of women, come in quickly
> to Sir John. He is so shaked with a
> burning quotidian fever, that it is
> most lamentable to behold. Sweet men, come to him.

She leaves them and the sobering thought of the old knight throws a renewed melancholy over the company, who know the full bitter truth of their rejection by the King. Out of the maudlin silence **Pistol** speaks for all of them.

> PISTOL
> Poor Sir John, a good portly man i'faith.

Caught in the flood of remembrance, he turns his head towards the fireplace and his expression changes as we hear, as if in a dream:

FALSTAFF
(Voice-over)
Ay, and of a cheerful look, a pleasing eye
and a most noble carriage.

Boar's Head Tavern: night (flashback)

We cut to reveal the great frame of **Falstaff,** standing by the roaring
fire, laughing and throwing wide his arms to greet the now happy
Pistol, Nym and **Bardolph.** They take their seats eagerly to listen
to the great man holding court. After the first cheerful outburst
he now assumes a mock serious melancholy.

FALSTAFF
But do I not dwindle? My skin hangs about me
like an old lady's loose gown.

As the assembled group roars with laughter, **Falstaff** casts an
accusatory eye over them.

FALSTAFF
Company, villainous company have been the spoil
of me.

As another roar goes up, **Mistress Quickly** and the **Boy** rush in to
be enveloped by the great man, then sit down beside him to listen
as **Falstaff** valiantly fights the jeering and delighted dissent.

FALSTAFF
I was as virtuous as a gentleman need to be,

33

virtuous enough: swore little, diced not above
seven days a week, went to a bawdy house not above
once in the quarter – of an hour; paid money I
borrowed – three or four times, lived well and in
good compass.

The speech has been greeted with the derisory laughter it deserves.

BARDOLPH
Why, you are so fat, Sir John, that you must
needs be out of all compass.

FALSTAFF
Do thou amend thy face and I'll amend my life.

This glorious put-down is not met with good grace from **Bardolph**,
who moves away from the table. **Falstaff** is not deterred and as he
looks around, smiling, a new laugh is heard.

FALSTAFF
Hal! Hal!

We follow the surprised and delighted **Falstaff** as he moves in front
of the fireplace to greet **Prince Hal**, soon to be **Henry V**, with an
enormous hug.

FALSTAFF
If sack and sugar be a fault, then God help the wicked.
If to be old and merry is a sin, if to be fat is
to be hated ... But no my good lord, when thou art King,
banish Pistol, banish Bardolph, banish Nym, but sweet
Jack Falstaff, valiant Jack Falstaff and therefore
more valiant being as he is old Jack Falstaff, banish
not him thy Harry's company, banish plump Jack and
banish all the world.

As we cut to close up on the **King-to-be**, the smiling features turn
cold. He holds his look and we hear, in a chilling and ghostly
tone:

HAL
(Voice-over)
I do. I will.

We cut back to the shocked features of **Falstaff**, massively hurt.

FALSTAFF
But ... we have heard the chimes at midnight,
Master Harry.

34   Then, almost inaudibly, with the last painful ounce of pleading:

FALSTAFF
Jesus, the days that we have seen.
HAL
(Voice-over)
I know thee not, old man.

Falstaff backs away from him and slowly, painfully, closes his eyes.

Pistol and Nym who have been watching this exchange now slowly turn to look at each other and as they do we cut back to:

Boar's Head Tavern: day (real time)
The two men face each other in front of the cold morning fire. Bardolph sits down between them. They are still deep in this depressing recollection.

NYM
The king hath run bad humours on the knight.
PISTOL
Nym, thou hast spoke the right;
His heart is fracted and corroborate.
NYM
The king is a good king: but it must be as it may; he passes some humours and careers.

And with that notable understatement perhaps heading the trio into a longer and even sadder discourse on former glories, Pistol, with the characteristic optimism of the born survivor, tries to change the atmosphere.

PISTOL
Let us condole the knight; for, lambkins, we will live!

Pistol lowers his head, unsure of the truth of this last statement, Nym and Bardolph even more doubtful.

DISSOLVE TO:

Sea Shore: day
The Chorus is standing on a grassy cliff edge, looking out to sea. He turns to look at the camera.

CHORUS
The French, advised by good intelligence

Of this most 'dreadful' preparation,
Shake in their fear and with pale policy
Seek to divert the English purposes.

He walks slowly towards the camera, revealing the top of the cliff
behind him.

CHORUS
O England! Model to thy inward greatness,
Like little body with a mighty heart,
What might'st thou do, that honour would thee do,
Were all thy children kind and natural!
But see, thy fault France hath in thee found out,
A nest of hollow bosoms, which he fills
With treacherous crowns; and three corrupted men.

He turns to look towards the cliff top and we cut closer to the
traitors who have now appeared, passing through frame as their
names are mentioned.

CHORUS
(Voice-over)
One, Richard Earl of Cambridge, and the second,
Henry Lord Scroop of Masham, and the third,
Sir Thomas Grey, knight, of Northumberland,

The **Chorus** turns back towards camera, the three traitors in the
distance, looking out towards France. As the **Chorus** moves on,
we follow him, revealing the sea beyond.

CHORUS
Have for the gilt of France, – O guilt indeed! –
Confirmed conspiracy with fearful France;
And by their hands this grace of kings must die,
Ere he take ship for France.
The traitors are agreed;
The king is set from London; and the scene
Is now transported, gentles, to Southampton;

As he walks away along the cliff edge, wrapping his scarf around
him against the cold sea air, beyond him we see the dramatic white
cliffs of the English coastline.

DISSOLVE TO:

Hostelry, Southampton: day

Through a spy-hole in a partition we see a gathering of the English
nobles in a small private hostelry room. **Gloucester** is studying a

map at the centre table. **Westmoreland** enters the shot to look through the hole at the men. We start to pull away to bring **Bedford** and **Exeter** into the foreground. **Bedford** is clearly frustrated by the King's failure to deal with the traitors. The atmosphere is tense and expectant.

BEDFORD
'Fore God his grace is bold to trust these traitors.
EXETER
They shall be apprehended by and by.
WESTMORELAND
How smooth and even they do bear themselves!
As if allegiance in their bosoms sat,
Crowned with faith and constant loyalty.

Erpingham now joins the group of worried nobles.

BEDFORD
The king hath note of all that they intend,
By interception which they dream not of.
EXETER
Nay, but the man that was his bedfellow,
Whom he hath dulled and cloyed with gracious favours,
That he should, for a foreign purse, so sell
His sovereign's life to death and treachery!

At this moment they hear the sound of the doors opening and all leap to attention as **Henry** enters the room, carrying maps and papers, the last-minute business before the departure for France. He stops at the centre table, surrounded by his men, the three traitors nearest to him. He signals for the doors to be bolted. He is calm and decisive, apparently unworried.

HENRY V
Now sits the wind fair and we will aboard.
My lord of Cambridge, and my kind lord of Masham,
And you, my gentle knight, give me your thoughts:
Think you not that the powers we bear with us
Will cut their passage through the force of France?

Scroop, the King's dearest friend, answers first.

SCROOP
No doubt, my liege, if each man do his best.
HENRY V
I doubt not that;
CAMBRIDGE
Never was monarch better feared and loved

Than is your majesty.
GREY
True.
HENRY V
We therefore have great cause of thankfulness.

And, as if to celebrate the fact:

HENRY V
Uncle of Exeter,
Enlarge the man committed yesterday
That railed against our person: we consider
It was excess of wine that set him on;
And on his more advice we pardon him.
SCROOP
That's mercy, but too much security:
Let him be punished, sovereign, lest example
Breed, by his sufferance, more of such a kind.
HENRY V
O, let us yet be merciful.
CAMBRIDGE
So may your highness, and yet punish too.
GREY
Sir,
You show great mercy, if you give him life
After the taste of much correction.

The **King** takes in their advice and then quietly, with gratitude for
their concern, and great compassion, he rejects it. All eyes are on
him. He speaks quietly but with conviction. There is no sign of
the storm to come.

HENRY V
Alas, your too much love and care of me
Are heavy orisons 'gainst this poor wretch!
If little faults, proceeding on distemper,
Shall not be winked at, how shall we stretch our eye
When capital crimes, chewed, swallowed and digested
Appear before us? We'll yet enlarge that man,
Though Cambridge, Scroop and Grey, in their dear care
And tender preservation of our person
Would have him punished.
And now to our French causes:

As he briskly changes the subject, he moves away from the traitors
to stand beside **Exeter.**

HENRY V

Who are the late commissioners?

CAMBRIDGE

I one, my lord:

Your highness bade me ask for it today.

SCROOP

So did you me, my liege.

GREY

And I, my royal sovereign.

HENRY V

(handing them the commissions)

Then, Richard Earl of Cambridge, there is yours;

There yours, Lord Scroop of Masham; and, sir knight

Grey of Northumberland, this same is yours:

The tone of voice changes as he delivers the following line directly
to them, with real edge.

HENRY V

Read them; and know, I know your worthiness.

As the men read their 'commissions', **Henry** continues briskly with
his business.

HENRY V
My lord of Westmoreland, Uncle Exeter,
We will aboard tonight.

The look on the faces of the three doomed men tells us that these
papers are not 'commissions'. Instead they are warrants for their
arrest and execution. **Henry** makes his move. He is now in deadly
earnest.

HENRY V
Why, how now, gentlemen!
What see you in those papers that you lose
So much complexion?
CAMBRIDGE
I do confess my fault,
And do submit me to your highness' mercy.
SCROOP
To which we all appeal.
HENRY V
The mercy that was quick in us of late
By your own counsel is suppressed and killed;
You must not dare, for shame, to talk of mercy;
For your own reasons turn into your bosoms,
As dogs upon their masters, worrying you.

The traitors panic in the realisation that their position is hopeless.
They make a sudden move for their swords. The nobles are ready.
Exeter grabs **Scroop** as he lunges for the **King**, violently pushing
him back against the wall. **Gloucester** deals with **Cambridge**.
York forces **Grey** to his knees, a knife at his throat.

Henry moves towards **Scroop**, the dearest and most treacherous
companion, the quiet rage is building.

HENRY V
See you, my princes and my noble peers,
These English monsters!
What shall I say to thee Lord Scroop? thou cruel,
Ingrateful, savage and inhuman creature!

On this, the emotion proves too much and he throws himself at
Scroop, grabbing him and throwing him down onto the table, to
deliver the following face to face. The **King** speaks with a mixture
of astonished anger and pity.

HENRY V
Thou that didst bear the key to all my counsels,
That knew'st the very bottom of my soul,

That almost might'st have coined me into gold,
Would'st thou have practised on me for thy use,
May it be possible that foreign hire
Could out of thee extract one spark of evil
That might annoy my finger? 'Tis so strange
That, though the truth of it stands off as gross
As black and white, my eye will scarcely see it.
So constant and unspotted didst thou seem,
That this thy fall hath left a kind of blot,
To mark the full-fraught man and best indued
With some suspicion.

This last line has been addressed to all the men gathered in the
room. A warning and a prophecy. **Henry**'s composure now
regained, with terrible sadness and grim resolution, he disposes of
the prisoners.

HENRY V
I will weep for thee;
For this revolt of thine, methinks, is like
Another fall of man.

He pulls **Scroop** onto his feet and throws him against the wall,
Grey and **Cambridge** are forced to follow. **Exeter** now takes over
the proceedings. He walks over to the traitors, and as he officially
arrests each man, he tears the insignia from round their necks.

EXETER
I arrest thee of high treason, by the name of
Richard Earl of Cambridge.
I arrest thee of high treason, by the name of
Thomas Grey, knight, of Northumberland.
I arrest thee of high treason, by the name of
Henry Lord Scroop of Masham.

He hits **Scroop** across the face in disgust and moves away as **Henry**
takes over.

HENRY V
Hear your sentence.
You have conspired against our royal person,
Joined with an enemy proclaimed and from his coffers
Received the golden earnest of our death;
Wherein you would have sold your king to slaughter
His princes and his peers to servitude,
His subjects to oppression and contempt,
And his whole kingdom into desolation.
Get you therefore hence,
Poor miserable wretches, to your death;
The taste whereof, God of his mercy give
You patience to endure, and true repentance
Of all your dear offences. Bear them hence.

As the traitors are marshalled away, **Henry** once again has to fight
his natural human instinct. He somewhere finds the force to
galvanise his generals. This latest test has been passed with flying
colours, as far as they're concerned, but at a great personal cost,
which we can read on the strained features. Nevertheless:

HENRY V
Now, lords, for France; the enterprise whereof
Shall be to you, as us, like glorious.
Since God so graciously hath brought to light
This dangerous treason lurking in our way.

Cheerly to sea; the signs of war advance:
No king of England if not king of France.

He leads the way out of the hostelry and to the waiting ship for
France.

DISSOLVE TO:

Boar's Head Tavern, Falstaff's Bedroom: night

Candlelight, which we move past to reveal in profile the dead face
of Falstaff. For a few moments we see Mistress Quickly lean over
him, her face drained of all emotion. She moves slowly away and
we remain on the great head before we cut to:

Boar's Head Tavern: night

The Boy picks up his small bundle of possessions from beside the
fireplace and moves over to join Pistol, Nym and Bardolph sitting
disconsolately on the stairs. Mistress Quickly trudges slowly down
to join them, finally sitting on the step next to Pistol. Their mood
is of great sadness. A great spirit has passed away and they must
leave for France.

MISTRESS QUICKLY
Prithee, honey-sweet husband, let me
bring thee to Staines.
PISTOL
            (plainly and uncharacteristically moved)
No; for my manly heart doth yearn.
Bardolph, be blithe; Nym, rouse thy vaunting veins:
Boy, bristle thy courage up: for Falstaff is dead,
And we must yearn therefore.
BARDOLPH
Would I were with him, wheresome 'er he is,
either in heaven or in hell!
MISTRESS QUICKLY
Nay, sure he's not in hell: he's in Arthur's
bosom, if ever a man went to Arthur's bosom.
He made a finer end and went away an it had
been any Christian child; he parted even
just between twelve and one, even at the
turning of the tide; for after I saw him
fumble with the sheets and play with flowers
and smile upon his fingers' ends, I knew there
was but one way; for his nose was as sharp

43

as a pen, and he babbled of green fields.
'How now, Sir John?' quoth I: 'what, man!
be of good cheer.' So he cried out 'God, God,
God!' three or four times; now I, to comfort
him, bid him he should not think of God, I
hoped there was no need to trouble himself
with any such thoughts yet. He bade me
put more clothes on his feet; I put my hand
into the bed and felt them, and they were as
cold as any stone; and then I felt to his knees
and so upward, and upward, and all was as
cold as any stone.

We have moved in close on **Mistress Quickly,** on the pain and
sadness in her eyes. She breaks down in tears. **Nym** changes the
mood as we move out to a wider shot of the group.

> NYM
> They say he cried out for sack.
> MISTRESS QUICKLY
> > (laughing in spite of herself)
> Ay, that he did.
> BARDOLPH
> And of women.
> MISTRESS QUICKLY
> > (mock indignant)
> Nay, that he did not.
> BOY
> Yes, that he did; said they were devils
> incarnate.
> MISTRESS QUICKLY
> He could never abide carnation. 'Twas
> a colour he never liked.
> BOY
> He said once, the devil would have him
> about women.
> MISTRESS QUICKLY
> He did in some sort handle women; but then
> he was rheumatic, and talked of the whore of
> Babylon.
> BOY
> Do you remember he saw a flea stick
> upon Bardolph's nose, and he said it was
> a black soul burning in hell?
> BARDOLPH
> Well, the fuel is gone that maintained
> that fire; that's all the riches I
> got in his service.

They can linger no more. The mood of melancholic recollection
must gently be broken.

> NYM
> Shall we shog? The king will be gone
> from Southampton.

Nym, the **Boy** and **Bardolph** get up and move to pick up their
things. **Pistol** and **Mistress Quickly** are left on the stairs; after a

moment she walks slowly over to the **Boy** to hug first him, and then Bardolph.

BARDOLPH
Farewell, Hostess.

She kisses him on the cheek and moves on to take her leave of **Nym.** He shies away from her kiss.

NYM
I cannot kiss, that is the humour of
it; but adieu.

He takes off the leather bracelet he wears and gives it to her. **Nym** leads them quickly away down the stairs, towards the door, **Pistol** and **Mistress Quickly** bringing up the rear. The couple stop at the top of the stairs. There is too much to say. Only the commonplace will do.

PISTOL
Let housewifery appear; keep close,
I thee command.
MISTRESS QUICKLY
Farewell.

Pistol moves down the stairs to follow the others who are waiting. He turns at the bottom for one last look at his wife.

MISTRESS QUICKLY
Adieu.

Pistol turns and leaves. We move very close on the tired and tear-stained face of **Mistress Quickly** as she turns away in her own quiet despair.

DISSOLVE TO:

A map, the sea route of the English ships from Southampton, across the Channel and on to Rouen, home of the French court. Over this we hear, in quiet, compassionate tones:

CHORUS
(Voice-over)
Follow, follow!
For who is he, whose chin is but enriched
With one appearing hair, that will not follow
These culled and choice-drawn cavaliers to France?

French Palace, Courtroom: night

The haunted face of the King of France. As the camera moves
away from him and around the court, we see the assembled group
of French nobles. The **Constable** of France, the Dukes of **Orleans**,
Berri and **Bretagne** and the **Dauphin**.

> FRENCH KING
> Thus comes the English with full power
> upon us;
> And more that carefully it us concerns
> To answer royally in our defences.
> Therefore the Dukes of Berri and of Bretagne,
> Of Brabant and of Orleans, shall make forth,
> And you Prince Dauphin,

The **Dauphin**, young, intelligent and arrogant interrupts his father.

> DAUPHIN
> My most redoubted father,
> It is most meet we arm us 'gainst the foe;
> For peace itself should not so dull a kingdom,
> But that defences, musters, preparations,
> Should be maintained, assembled and collected,
> As were a war in expectation.

He addresses the following to the whole court as if to convince
the other French generals of his belief and intention. Perhaps they
need to be convinced that this apparently foppish youth, cosy and
comfortable in the opulence of the French court (a marked
contrast to the English one), is capable of more than idle talk.

> DAUPHIN
> Therefore, I say 'tis meet we all go forth
> To view the sick and feeble parts of France;
> And let us do it with no show of fear;
> No with no more than if we heard that England
> Were busied with a Whitsun morris-dance:
> For, my good liege, she is so idly king'd
> By a vain, giddy, shallow, humorous youth,
> That fear attends her not.

The **Constable**, fair-minded and shrewd, must intervene. He may
enjoy the same arrogance and belief in French supremacy but he
has a more cautious respect for the English King, free from the
Dauphin's more personal hostility.

> CONSTABLE
> O peace, Prince Dauphin!

You are too much mistaken in this king.
Question your grace the late ambassadors,
With what great state he heard their embassy,
How well supplied with noble counsellors,
How modest in exception, and withal
How terrible in constant resolution.

Friction between the **Dauphin** and the other nobles is clear.

DAUPHIN
Well, 'tis not so, my lord high constable;
But though we think it so, it is no matter:
In cases of defence 'tis best to weigh
The enemy more mighty than he seems.

The **King** steps in with his own deeply-felt opinion of their
adversary. During this speech the remote and terrible haunted
expression returns, teetering on the thin line between fear and
madness.

FRENCH KING
Think we King Harry strong;
And, princes, look you strongly arm to meet him.
For he is bred out of that bloody strain
That haunted us in our familiar paths;
Witness our too much memorable shame
When Cressy battle fatally was struck,
And all our princes captived by the hand
Of that black name, Edward, Black Prince of Wales;
This is a stem
Of that victorious stock; and let us fear
The native mightiness and fate of him.

Caught in some terrible flood of remembrance, the **King** sinks into
a quiet reverie, burying his face in his hands. He is watched
anxiously by the Princes.

Montjoy arrives.

MONTJOY
Ambassadors from Harry King of England
Do crave admittance to your majesty.
FRENCH KING
Go, and bring them.

Montjoy exits and the **King** turns to face his court.

FRENCH KING
You see this case is hotly followed, friends.

The **Dauphin** moves swiftly to rally his worried father.

DAUPHIN
Good my sovereign,
Take up the English short, and let them know
Of what a monarchy you are the head.

The **Constable** stands up as if to intervene, but the **Dauphin** will
not be stopped.

DAUPHIN
Self-love, my liege, is not so vile a sin
As self-neglecting.

Before the **Dauphin** can continue, **Montjoy** returns bringing with
him **Exeter** in full armour. **Exeter** is resolute, dignified, defiant.
This martial entrance into a court so very different in atmosphere
is disturbing. The English obviously mean business. **Exeter** stands
at the far end of the court, opposite the **King**.

FRENCH KING
From our brother England?
EXETER
From him; and thus he greets your majesty.
He wills you, in the name of God almighty,
That you divest yourself, and lay apart
The borrowed glories that by gift of heaven,
By law of nature and of nations, 'longs
To him and to his heirs; namely, the crown.
Willing you overlook this pedigree;

Montjoy hands the **King** a document.

EXETER
And when you find him evenly derived
From his most famed of famous ancestors,
Edward the Third, he bids you then resign
Your crown and kingdom, indirectly held
From him the native and true challenger.

The **King** has not looked at the document instead, knowing its
contents, he hands it to the **Constable**.

FRENCH KING
Or else what follows?

The French Princes, surprised by this question, look around
nervously waiting for the reply.

EXETER
Bloody constraint; for if you hide the crown

Even in your heart there will he rake for it:
Therefore in fierce tempest is he coming
In thunder and in earthquake like a Jove,
That, if requiring fail, he will compel;
This is claim, his threatening and my message;
Unless the 'Dolphin' be in presence here,
To whom expressly I bring greeting too.
DAUPHIN
For the *Dauphin*,
I stand here for him;
      (moving towards **Exeter**)
What to him from England?

The smile on the **Dauphin's** face is wiped quickly away by **Exeter's** reply.

EXETER
Scorn and defiance; slight regard, contempt,
And anything that might not misbecome
The mighty sender, doth he prize you at.
Thus says my king.
DAUPHIN
Say, if my father render fair return,
It is against my will, for I desire
Nothing but odds with England: and to that end
As matching to his youth and vanity
I did present him with the Paris-balls.
EXETER
He'll make your Paris Louvre shake for it.
And be assured, you'll find a difference,
As we his subjects have in wonder found,
Between the promise of his greener days
And these he masters now.

The **King** defiantly and regally dismisses **Exeter**.

FRENCH KING
Tomorrow shall you know our mind at full.

Exeter bows and turns to leave the court. The **King** slowly closes his eyes, the haunted expression returns. Over this we hear the increasingly excited voice of the **Chorus**.

CHORUS
(Voice-over)
Thus with imagined wing our swift scene flies

DISSOLVE TO:

Walls and Breach, Harfleur: night

The huge breach at Harfleur. Noise. The sounds of battle.
Explosions. The movement of soldiers passing to and fro. The
Chorus continues, his speech is urgent, breathless as if he too were
caught up in the battle.

> CHORUS
> (Voice-over)
> **In motion of no less celerity**
> **Than that of thought.**

Trench near Battlefield, Harfleur: night

Now we cut close on the **Chorus**, he is caught up wildly in the
excitement of the gunfire, smoke and explosions.

> CHORUS
> **Work, work your thoughts and in them see a siege.**
> **Behold the ordnance on their carriages,**
> **With fatal mouths gaping on girded Harfleur.**
> **Suppose the ambassador from the French comes back;**
> **Tells Harry that the king does offer him**
> **Katherine his daughter; and with her, to dowry,**
> **Some petty and unprofitable dukedoms:**
> **The offer likes him not; and the nimble gunner**
> **With linstock now the devilish cannon touches**
> **And down goes all before them!**

As he yells this last line and moves away, another massive
explosion is heard and we cut to:

Walls and Breach, Harfleur: night

Through the dispersing smoke we see the panicked retreat of the
English army from the exploding breach in the massive city wall.
Making their desperate way are **Fluellen, Gower, Jamy** and
Macmorris, Pistol, Bardolph, Nym, Boy, Bates, Williams, Court
and other soldiers.

Exeter is yelling them out, as the other nobles, **Bedford,
Westmoreland, Erpingham** and **Gloucester** follow the soldiers, all
making their way through the deep mud of the battlefield to the
relative safety of the trench.

Back lit silhouetted against the furnace, sword brandished, appears
Henry on his horse. The horse rears up in the centre of the breach
and as it comes down to the ground:

HENRY V
Once more unto the breach, dear friends, once more,
Or close the wall up with our English dead.

These words, screamed heroically from **Henry**'s vantage point,
have done nothing to stem the tide of English soldiers running
away. He gallops back to join the main body of his retreating men,
now gathered in and around the trench, exhausted or injured. As
he delivers his speech of passionate persuasion with smoke, fire
and battle raging all around him, more and more men join the
group.

HENRY V
In peace there's nothing so becomes a man
As modest stillness and humility;
But when the blast of war blows in our ears,
Then imitate the action of the tiger.
Stiffen the sinews, summon up the blood,

Disguise fair nature with hard-favoured rage:
Then lend the eye a terrible aspect;
Let it pry through the portage of the head
Like the brass cannon; let the brow o'erwhelm it
As fearfully as doth a galled rock
O'erhang and jutty his confounded base,
Swilled with the wild and wasteful ocean.
Now set the teeth and stretch the nostril wide,
Hold hard the breath and bend up every spirit
To his full height! On, on, you noblest English!

Another huge explosion fills the air as the **King** continues.

HENRY V
Dishonour not your mothers: now attest
That those whom you called fathers did beget you.
And you, good yeomen,

As he makes the following appeal directly to the men concerned, **Williams** draws his sword.

HENRY V
Whose limbs were made in England, show us here
The mettle of your pasture; let us swear
That you are worth your breeding; which I doubt not;
For there is none of you so mean and base
That hath not noble lustre in your eyes.
I see you stand like greyhounds in the slips,
Straining upon the start. The game's afoot:

The army now wild-eyed and eager.

HENRY V
Follow your spirit; and upon this charge
Cry, 'God for Harry, England, and Saint George!'

Another explosion as **Henry's** horse once again rears up, before he turns and rides off back towards the breach. The army scream their battle cry and follow their King towards the wall.

Trench, Harfleur: night

The noise and smoke persist but one group remains cowering in the trench, urging the last few men up towards the battlefield, before turning away to make their escape. **Nym**, **Bardolph** and **Pistol** run straight into **Captain Fluellen**.

Most loyal of the King's soldiers, a fierce, eccentric disciplinarian, Welsh to his very bones, he chases the three low-lifers out of the trench towards the battlefield.

FLUELLEN
Up to the breach, you dogs! Avaunt you cullions!

As the three move out, **Fluellen**'s attention is caught by an
explosion at the far end of the trench. **Captain Gower** is propelled
by the explosion into a large pool, but manages to pick himself
up and move on, calling the Welshman to him. They crouch next
to the temporarily sealed entrance to one of the English mine-
shafts, designed to tunnel under and blow up the Harfleur walls.

GOWER
Captain Fluellen, you must come presently
to the mines; the Duke of Gloucester would
speak with you.

FLUELLEN
Tell you the duke it is not so good
to come to the mines. For look you,
the mines is not accordng to the
disciplines of war. By Cheshu, I think
he will blow up all if there is not
better directions.

GOWER
The Duke of Gloucester, to whom the order
of the siege is given, is altogether
directed by an Irishman.

FLUELLEN
It is Captain Macmorris, is it not?

GOWER
I think it be.

FLUELLEN
By Cheshu, he is an ass in the world;
he has no more directions in the true
disciplines of the wars than is a puppy
dog.

As he speaks, two blackened faces emerge from the narrow opening
to the mine-shaft.

GOWER
Here he comes; and the Scots captain,
Captain Jamy, with him.

FLUELLEN
Ah now, Captain Jamy is a marvellous
valorous gentleman, that is certain.

An exhausted **Captain Jamy** is the first out, gratefully taking a drinking flask from **Fluellen**. A battle-blackened **Captain Macmorris** follows.

JAMY
I say good day, Captain Fluellen.
FLUELLEN
Good day to your worship, good
Captain James.
GOWER
How now, Captain Macmorris! Have you
quit the mines?
MACMORRIS
By Christ, la! The work is give over,
the trumpet sound the retreat. By my hand, 'tis ill done.

Macmorris is wild and apparently deranged. It's enough – even at such a time – to bring out the military pedant in **Fluellen**.

FLUELLEN
Captain Macmorris, I beseech you now, a
few disputations as partly touching the
disciplines of the war. Partly to satisfy
my opinion, and partly for the satisfaction
of my mind, as touching the direction of
the military discipline. That is the point.
MACMORRIS
It is no time to discourse, so Chrish
save me. The town is beseeched, and the
trumpet calls us to the breach, and we
talk and, by Chrish, do nothing.
JAMY
By the mass, ere these eyes of mine take
themselves to slumber I'll do good service,
or I'll lie in the ground for it.
FLUELLEN
Captain Macmorris, I think, look you,
under your correction, there is not many
of your nation –
MACMORRIS
What is my nation? Who talks of my nation
is a villain and a bastard and a knave
and a rascal –
FLUELLEN
Look you, if you take the matter otherwise

than it is meant, Captain Macmorris, per –
adventure I shall think you do not use
me with that affability as in discretion
you ought to use me, now look you; being as
good a man as yourself.
MACMORRIS
I do not know you so good a man as myself,
so Chrish save me, I will cut off you head.

As **Macmorris** lunges for **Fluellen**, their attention is diverted by
the arrival of the rest of the English army, once again in retreat.
As they pour over into the trench we see **Henry** ride up to assess
the situation. Apart from the rivalry of factions within the army,
the siege of Harfleur is now going disastrously wrong, costing
more and more men. The glorious campaign that was to have
been is crumbling. The resilience of Harfleur seems unbreakable.

Henry turns his horse away determinedly, and rides back towards
the breach, where all is now eerily quiet and still, apart from the
crackling of fires burning inside.

Bloodstained, filthy, and as if possessed by some demon, the **King**
unleashes an ultimatum to the timid **Governor** who appears on
the ramparts above the breach.

HENRY V
How yet resolves the governor of the town?
This is the latest parle we will admit;
Therefore to our best mercy give yourselves;
Or like to men proud of destruction
Defy us to our worst: for, as I am a soldier,
If I begin the battery once again,
I will not leave the half-achieved Harfleur
Till in her ashes she lie buried.

As **Henry** continues, the nervous and exhausted citizens of Harfleur
join the **Governor** on the ramparts – frightened children, women,
old men.

Henry's own soldiers, arrested by the display of almost
uncontrollable rage, watch from the trench.

HENRY V
Therefore, you men of Harfleur,
Take pity of your town and of your people,
Whiles yet the cool and temperate wind of grace
O'er blows the filthy and contagious clouds
Of heady murder, spoil and villainy.

If not, why in a moment look to see
The blind and bloody soldier with foul hand
Defile the locks of your shrill-shrieking daughters;
Your fathers taken by the silver beards,
And their most reverend heads dashed to the walls;
Your naked infants spitted upon pikes,
Whiles the mad mothers with their howls confused
Do break the clouds.

A last pause. This is no idle threat.

HENRY V
What say you?
Will you yield, and this avoid?
Or, guilty in defence, be thus destroyed?

The **Governor**, shaken, makes his response.

GOVERNOR
The Dauphin, of whose succours we entreated,
Returns us that his powers are not yet ready
To raise so great a siege. Therefore, dread king,
Enter our gates; dispose of us and ours;
For we no longer are defensible.

Henry closes his eyes in exhaustion and relief, then slowly turns
his horse and rides back towards his men.

He dismounts. The horse is led away as he meets **Exeter**. The rest
of the army moves slowly past them towards the city.

Henry addresses his uncle.

> HENRY V
> Go you and enter Harfleur; there remain
> And fortify it strongly 'gainst the French.

As **Exeter** starts to move out, **Henry** stops him and, with a complete change of tone, says:

> HENRY V
> Use mercy to them all.
> > (looking at a map)
> For us, dear uncle,
> The winter coming on and sickness growing
> Upon our soldiers, we will retire to Calais.

The **general** shoots him a surprised glance. The march to Calais is obviously an open gesture of defiance to the French, but it means a march of two hundred miles for which a sorely depleted army is ill-equipped. There is no arguing with the **King**'s tone or look.

> HENRY V
> Tonight in Harfleur will we be your guest:
> Tomorrow for the march are we addressed.

As they start to move out, **Henry** stumbles with some sudden pain. **Exeter** catches him and helps him away towards the city walls. As smoke fills the screen we:

> DISSOLVE TO:

Princess Katherine's Bedroom: day

At the bars of her doves' lattice-work enclosure we see **Princess Katherine** of France, gently waking the caged birds in the bright morning light.

As she turns away from the peaceful doves and moves into the room she calls to her gentlewoman, **Alice,** who enters immediately. As the **Princess** sits down at her dressing-table, and **Alice** begins to comb her hair, **Katherine** resigns herself to the fact that she must learn to speak English.

KATHERINE
Alice, tu as été en Angleterre,
et tu parles bien le langage.
ALICE
Un peu, madame.
KATHERINE
Je te prie, m'enseignez; il faut que
j'apprenne à parler. Comment appellez-
vous la main en Anglais?
ALICE
La main? Elle est appellée de hand.
KATHERINE
De hand. Et les doigts?
ALICE
Les doigts? Ma foi, j'oublie les
doigts mais je me souviendrai. Les
doigts? Je pense qu'ils sont appellés
de fingres.
KATHERINE
La main, de hand; les doigts, de
fingres. Je pense que je suis le bon
écolier. J'ai gagné deux mots d'Anglais
vitement.
Comment appellez-vous les ongles?
ALICE
Les ongles? nous les appellons de nails.
KATHERINE
De nails. Écoutez; dites moi si je parle
bien: de hand, de fingres et de nails.
ALICE
C'est bien dit madame; il est fort bon
Anglais.

KATHERINE
Dites–moi l'Anglais pour le bras.
ALICE
De arm, madame.
KATHERINE
Et le coude?
ALICE
D'elbow.
KATHERINE
D'elbow.

Katherine jumps up and runs towards the doves, Alice following her, delighting in the fun of the exchange.

KATHERINE
Je m'en fais la répétition
de tous les mots que vous m'avez
appris dès à présent.
ALICE
Il est trop difficile, madame, comme
je pense.
KATHERINE
Excusez-moi, Alice; écoutez; De hand,
de fingres, de nails, de arma, de bilbow.
ALICE
D'elbow, madame.
KATHERINE
O Seigneur Dieu! Je m'en oublie;
d'elbow.

In a gesture of mock annoyance, Katherine sits sharply down beside the birds to continue her lesson.

KATHERINE
Comment appellez-vous le col?
ALICE
De nick, madame.
KATHERINE
De nick. Et le menton?
ALICE
De chin.
KATHERINE
De sin. Le col, de nick; le menton,
de sin.
ALICE
Sauf votre honneur, en verité,

> vous prononcez les mots aussi droit
> que les natifs d'Angleterre.

Katherine leaps up, laughs, and flits across the room towards her bed.

KATHERINE
Je ne doute point d'apprendre par la grace
de Dieu, et en peu de temps.
ALICE
N'avez vous pas déjà oublié ce que je
vous ai enseignée?

Katherine closes the lace at the end of the bed, making a curtain between herself and **Alice**, so that she can 'perform' this newly acquired language to her delighted teacher.

KATHERINE
Non, je réciterai à vous promptement.
         (As her arm appears through the curtain)
De hand, de fingres, de mails –
ALICE
De nails, madame.
KATHERINE
         (mimicking Alice)
De nails, madame.
De arm, de bolbow.
ALICE
Sauf votre honneur, d'elbow.

Katherine pokes her head out from behind the curtain.

KATHERINE
Ainsi dis-je: d'elbow, de nick, et de sin.

The two women sit down facing each other.

KATHERINE
Comment appellez-vous le pied et la robe?
ALICE
         (in more hushed tones)
Le foot, madame, et le coun.
KATHERINE
         (whispering)
Le foot et le coun.

They start to laugh at the sound of these words, translating them into startlingly bawdy French.

KATHERINE
O Seigneur Dieu!

Ils sont les mots de son mauvais,
corruptible, gros et impudique, et
non pour les dames d'honneur d'user.
Je ne voudrais prononcer ces mots devant
les seigneurs de France, pour tout le
monde. Foh! Le foot et le coun.
Néanmoins je réciterai une autre fois ma
leçon ensemble:

Once again, the **Princess** is on her feet, delighting in this delicious naughtiness, and dancing around the room, reciting the words on her way to the door to her bedroom, as she gently teases **Alice**.

KATHERINE
De hand, de fingres, de nails, de arma,
de bilelelelbow, de nick, de sin,
de foot et le coun.
ALICE
Excellent, madame!

At this moment **Katherine** throws open the door only to see her father the **King** of **France**, surrounded by his council of war, the **Dauphin, Constable, Orleans, Berri**, and **Bretagne**. Their mood is grim and **Katherine** is immediately quiet and serious. The men move on towards the Council Chamber and the **Princess**, slowly, sadly closes the door.

French King's Council Chamber: day

In huge close-up, the **French King**, head in hands, slowly raises his eyes and we see the familiar haunted expression. He looks around at the assembled nobles, **Constable, Orleans, Berri** and **Bretagne**. The **Dauphin** is close to the **King**, and very agitated. This war council wants action now.

FRENCH KING
'Tis certain he hath passed the river
Somme.
CONSTABLE
And if he be not fought withal, my lord,
Let us not live in France.
DAUPHIN
Normans, but bastard Normans, Norman
bastards!
CONSTABLE
Where have they this mettle?

Is not their climate foggy, raw and dull?
ORLEANS
O, for honour of our land.
DAUPHIN
By faith and honour,
Our madams mock at us, and plainly say
Our mettle is bred out:

The **Dauphin**, angry, moves away from the throne to sit down and
face the **King**.

DAUPHIN
And they will give
Their bodies to the lust of English youth
To new-store France with bastard warriors.

The **Princes** are united. The **King** has no choice.

> FRENCH KING
> Where is Montjoy the Herald? Speed him hence;
> Let him greet England with our sharp defiance.
> Up, princes, and with spirit of honour edged
> More sharper than your swords, hie to the field:
> Bar Harry England, that sweeps through our land
> With pennons painted in the blood of Harfleur:
> Go down upon him, you have power enough,
> And in a captive chariot into Rouen
> Bring him our prisoner.
> CONSTABLE
> This becomes the great.
> Sorry I am his numbers are so few,
> His soldiers sick and famished in their march,
> For I am sure when he shall see our army
> He'll drop his heart into the sink of fear,
> And for achievement offer us his ransom.
> FRENCH KING
> Therefore, lord constable, haste on Montjoy.

As the **Princes** rise to leave, the **King** stops the **Dauphin** with unexpected authority.

> FRENCH KING
> Prince Dauphin, you shall stay with us
> in Rouen.

The **Dauphin** pleads with his father in a tone of quiet desperation.

> DAUPHIN
> Not so, I do beseech your majesty.
> FRENCH KING
> Be patient, for you shall remain with us.

The **King** silences the **Dauphin** with the sharpness of this response, and with a similar strength of purpose turns his attentions to the rest of the **Princes**.

> FRENCH KING
> Now forth, lord constable and princes all,
> And quickly bring us word of England's fall.

French Countryside and River Crossing: day

We cut straight into a montage sequence of the bedraggled **English Army** on the march, intercut with a map of their route. It is pouring with rain and the road deep in mud. They are exhausted. No time to rest after the battle at Harfleur, they are now marching all day with everything against them. They have tried to cross numerous rivers to march north towards Calais, but their way is being blocked at each attempt by the **French Army**, who have followed them step for step on the opposite side of the river.

We see many of the principal English soldiers, **Nym, Jamy**, the **Boy** falling face first into the mud, helped up by **Williams, Macmorris, Court** and many more.

At last they find a place to cross. **Henry** leads his men past a cart stuck in the river, the foot soldiers follow and then the nobles on horseback, **Gloucester, Bedford**, etc. This is not a victorious army on the march, but a sick and depleted band of men. There is little hope of reaching Calais without a major confrontation with the vastly superior French forces.

Muddy Track: day

The rain has stopped briefly, and **Captain Gower**, part of the advance party, is studying a map. From the distance the sound of horse's hooves and **Captain Fluellen** rides along the muddy track towards the English Captain.

Fluellen had been sent ahead to check the position of the forward army led by **Exeter**. He has ridden hard to report his findings. Exhausted, he dismounts.

> GOWER
> How now, Captain Fluellen, come you from the bridge?
> Is the Duke of Exeter safe?
> FLUELLEN
> He is not – God be praised and blessed! – any
> hurt in the world, but keeps the bridge most
> valiantly with excellent discipline.

The two **Captains** embrace. They are distracted by the approach of **Pistol** from the nearby bushes. He is breathless and agitated.

> PISTOL
> Captain, I thee beseech to do me favours:
> the Duke of Exeter doth love thee well.
> FLUELLEN
> Ay, I praise God; and I have merited
> some love at his hands.
> PISTOL
> Bardolph, a soldier firm and sound of heart,

of buxom valour, hath by cruel fate,
and giddy fortune's furious fickle wheel,

Fluellen knows what's coming, and cuts him off sharply.

FLUELLEN
Touching your patience, Ancient Pistol. Fortune
is an excellent moral.
PISTOL
Fortune is Bardolph's foe and frowns on him;
for he hath stolen a pax and hanged must he be.
Therefore go speak, the duke will hear thy voice:
    (desperately grabbing **Fluellen**'s arm)
Speak, captain, for his life, and I will thee requite.
FLUELLEN
Ancient Pistol, I do partly understand your meaning.
PISTOL
Why then, rejoice therefore.
FLUELLEN
It is not a thing to rejoice at: for
if, look you, he were my brother, I would
desire the duke to use his good pleasure
and put him to execution; for discipline
ought to be used.

At this moment **Fluellen** sees **Henry** and the rest of the army
marching towards them. **Pistol** gives in.

PISTOL
Die and be damned: and figo for thy friendship.

He hurries towards the approaching army who come to a halt as
the **King** dismounts and **Fluellen** approaches, ready to report to
the King.

HENRY V
How now, Fluellen! Cam'st thou from the bridge?
FLUELLEN
Ay, so please your majesty. The Duke of Exeter
has very gallantly maintained the bridge.
HENRY V
What men have you lost, Fluellen?
FLUELLEN
I think the duke hath lost never a man.

The relief on the **King**'s face is obvious, but as **Fluellen** smiles, he
turns at the sound of an approaching cart. Through the mist we

see it is carrying the kneeling figure of **Bardolph**, now a prisoner, with **Exeter** beside him, holding a rope.

> FLUELLEN
> ... but one, that is like to be executed
> for robbing a church; one Bardolph, if
> your majesty know the man?

At the sound of this familiar name, the colour drains from **Henry's** face as he turns to see his former companion and friend. As **Fluellen** continues, the cart is brought to a halt beside a tree, in front of **Henry**.

> FLUELLEN
> His face is all bubukles and whelks and
> knobs and flames of fire; and his lips
> blows at his nose, and it is like a coal
> of fire sometimes blue and sometimes red;
> but his nose is executed and his fire's out.

Bardolph's nose has indeed been split open as an intermediary punishment.

Once again, through the unknowing **Fluellen**, a public trial of strength is provided for the **King**. Watched by his sodden soldiers, he must enforce his decree that any form of theft or pillage of the French countryside will be punished by death. Any favouritism or sentiment shown here will be disastrous for discipline amongst these poor soldiers.

The cost to the **King** is enormous as he gives the nod to **Exeter** who pulls **Bardolph** to his feet, throwing the rope over the overhanging branch of the tree and putting the noose around the old man's neck. We see **Bardolph's** frightened look as the rope is pulled tight and then **Henry's** distressed but unflinching stare. Over this we first hear and then cut to:

Boar's Head Tavern: night (flashback)

Bardolph in happier days taking part in a drinking contest with **Falstaff**. As the two men pour back the ale, they are egged on by the other members of the Boar's Head group, **Nym**, the **Boy**, **Pistol**, **Mistress Quickly**, and other customers. On the other side of the room is the young **Hal**, enjoying the event.

Bardolph watches **Falstaff** out of the corner of his eye and, at a crucial moment, digs him in the ribs, causing him to spill his jug and stop the contest. They all fall on **Bardolph** and grab him around the neck in mock outrage. With his head completely

encircled in their arms, he appeals to **Hal** through his laughter:

> BARDOLPH
> **Do not, when thou are king, hang a thief.**

The smile on **Hal**'s face drops away.

> HAL
> **No, thou shalt.**

From the shocked face of **Bardolph** at his future King's response
we:

DISSOLVE TO:

Muddy Track: day (real time)

The stricken and bloody face of the condemned man, his head in
the noose.

Henry, his eyes filled with tears, slowly signals to **Exeter**. The
Duke kicks **Bardolph** off as the cart is pulled away and a group
of soldiers pull on the rope and drag him up into the air.

The **King** stares at the ugly death throes of his former friend. Tears
stain his cheeks. At last the writhing stops and in a thick silence

Henry forces out the following.

HENRY V
We would have all such offenders so cut off.
And we give express charge that in our
marches through the country there be
nothing compelled from the villages,
nothing taken but paid for, none of the
French upbraided or abused in disdainful
language; for when lenity and cruelty
play for a kingdom, the gentler gamester
is the soonest winner.

The sound of a galloping horse disturbs the ghostly calm. Riding
towards them is **Montjoy**. He comes to a halt beside the hanging
body of **Bardolph**, looking up at it, uneasy, before delivering his
message.

MONTJOY
Thus says my king: Say thou to Harry of England:
though we seemed dead, we did but sleep.
Tell him we could have rebuked him at Harfleur.
Now we speak and our voice is imperial:
England shall repent his folly.
Bid him therefore consider of his ransom,
which must proportion the losses we have borne
which in weight to re-answer,
his pettiness would bow under. To this add
defiance: and tell him for conclusion
he hath betrayed his followers whose
condemnation is pronounced.
So far my king and master, so much my office.
HENRY V
What is thy name?
MONTJOY.
Montjoy
HENRY V
Thou dost thy office fairly. Turn thee back,
And tell thy king I do not seek him now,
But could be willing to march on to Calais
Without impeachment.
Go therefore, tell thy master here I am;
My ransom is this frail and worthless trunk,
My army but a weak and sickly guard;
Yet, God before, tell him we will come on,

Though France himself and such another neighbour
Stand in our way. So Montjoy fare you well,
The sum of all our answer is but this:
We would not seek a battle as we are;
Nor, as we are, we say we will not shun it:
So tell your master.
MONTJOY
I shall deliver so. Thanks to your majesty.

Montjoy hesitates a moment, impressed by the unexpected strength
of this English King. He turns and rides back the way he came.

As Henry watches the Herald, Gloucester rides up to stop beside
the king slightly away from the rest of the men.

GLOUCESTER (confidentially)
I hope they will not come upon us now.
HENRY V
We are in God's hands, brother, not in theirs.

As if in answer to this, the rain begins to pour again. Henry turns
to face his army as they attempt to protect themselves from the
downpour.

HENRY V
March to the bridge; it now draws towards night:
Beyond the river we'll encamp ourselves.

Then, almost to himself:

HENRY V
And on tomorrow bid them march away.

As Henry moves away, the army begin to continue their journey,
having to make their way under the lifeless body of Bardolph,
and on up the muddy track. Henry, now on his horse, rejoins the
army ahead of the heavy carts, which are struggling through the
mud. The rain is unremitting as they make their way towards the
bridge.

From behind the tree where Bardolph hangs, the Chorus appears.
He glances up at the dead body before wrapping his coat tight
around him and addressing the camera. As he speaks, the light
seems to fade as if darkness is falling.

CHORUS
Now entertain conjecture of a time
When creeping murmur and the poring dark
Fills the wide vessel of the universe.

As he moves off, away from the body, we travel with him.

CHORUS
From camp to camp through the foul womb of the night,
The hum of either army stilly sounds,
That the fixed sentinels almost receive
The secret whispers of each other's watch:
Fire answers fire and through their paly flames
Each battle sees the other's umbered face;
Steed threatens steed, in high and boastful neighs
Piercing the night's dull ear; and from the tents
The armourers, accomplishing the knights,
With busy hammers closing rivets up,
Give dreadful note of preparation.
Proud of their numbers, and secure in soul,
The confident and over-lusty French
Do the low-rated English play at dice;
And chide the cripple tardy-gaited night
Who, like a foul and ugly witch, doth limp
so tediously away.

He now walks away along the muddy track, following the
stragglers of the English army who can be seen in the gloom ahead
of him.

DISSOLVE TO:

Constable's Pavilion: night

The ornate tent which is the Constable's Pavilion. We move along
it past a soldier on guard, and hear from inside:

CONSTABLE
(Voice-over)
I have the best armour in the world.
Would it were day.

ORLEANS
(Voice-over)
You have an excellent armour; but let my
horse have his due.

Constable's Pavilion: night

Inside the tent, the comparative luxury of the French nobles is
even more obvious. They are drinking from silver goblets, fur
rugs line the floor and couch.

ORLEANS
You have an excellent armour; but let my
horse have his due.

CONSTABLE
It is the best horse of Europe.

ORLEANS
Will it never be morning?

The **Dauphin**, unable to resist this gentle sparring, joins in with his customary zeal.

DAUPHIN
My lord of Orleans, and my lord high
constable, you talk of horse and armour?

Orleans tries to stop him before it is too late.

ORLEANS
You are as well provided of both as any
prince in the world.

Too late.

DAUPHIN
I will not change my horse with any that
treads but on four hoofs.

Warming to his theme, he begins to pace the tent. The **Constable** and **Orleans** glance at one another, their hostility for the **Dauphin** obvious.

DAUPHIN
When I bestride him I soar, I am a hawk.
He is pure air and fire and the
dull elements of earth and water never
appear in him, but only in patient
stillness while his rider mounts him.

The **Constable** has had enough of this hyperbole.

CONSTABLE
Indeed my lord, it is a most absolute and
excellent horse.

The emphasis of the **Constable**'s last word stops the **Dauphin**. Friction between the two is growing. A tense silence is broken by **Montjoy**.

MONTJOY
My lord constable, the armour in your tent
tonight, are those stars or suns upon it?

CONSTABLE
Stars, Montjoy.

DAUPHIN
Some of them will fall tomorrow. I hope.

77

This spleen is not lost on the **Constable** who fires right back.

> **CONSTABLE**
> And yet my sky shall not want.

The **Dauphin** becoming more and more restless and tense.

> **DAUPHIN**
> Will it never be day!
> I will trot tomorrow a mile, and my way
> shall be paved with English faces.

The **Constable** with even less patience now for the **Dauphin**'s arrogance.

> **CONSTABLE**
> I will not say so for fear I should be faced
> out of my way.

The two men stare at each other. The tension underlying their vigil is now explicit. The **Dauphin** decides to leave. He walks to the door of the tent.

> **DAUPHIN**
> I'll go arm myself.

As the **Dauphin** exits, **Orleans** attempts to lighten the atmosphere as he and the **Constable** move to look out of the tent door to the night outside.

> **ORLEANS**
> The Dauphin longs for morning.
> He longs to eat the English.
> **CONSTABLE**
> I think he will eat all he kills.
> **ORLEANS**
> He never did harm that I heard of.
> **CONSTABLE**
> Nor will do none tomorrow.

The **Constable** gazes out towards the English camp. Most confident, and yet most wary of the French princes. For all their supremacy, he knows they have a difficult fight on their hands tomorrow.

> **CONSTABLE**
> Would it were day. Alas! poor Harry of England, he longs not
> for the dawning as we do.
> **ORLEANS**
> If the English had any apprehension, they would run away.

Montjoy now joins them at the entrance to the tent. The only one of them to know the English well, his words carry a strange power.

MONTJOY
That island of England breeds very valiant
creatures.

The **Herald** leaves the tent and the **Princes** watch after him. The words are wisely spoken. A warning, but the French intend to win.

CONSTABLE
Now is it time to arm; come, shall we about it?
ORLEANS
It is now two o'clock: but, let me see, by ten
We shall have each a hundred Englishmen.

As the two confident **Princes** move back into the tent, the **Chorus** appears to take their places in the entrance and turns to face the camera.

CHORUS
The poor condemned English,
Like sacrifices, by their watchful fires
Sit patiently and inly ruminate
The morning's danger.

As he turns and closes the folds of the Constable's tent we:

DISSOLVE TO:

English Camp: night

The flames of a small fire and the starkness of the English camp.
Sitting in a group are the English nobles, **Exeter**, **Westmoreland**,
Erpingham, **York**. As **Gloucester** and **Bedford** stand to move away,
we start to widen out from the group, seeing **Fluellen** moving
around the camp. We pass **Williams**, **Court** and **Bates** around
another fire. Over this we hear:

CHORUS
(Voice-over)
… and their gesture sad.
Investing lank-lean cheeks and war-worn coats
Presenteth them unto the gazing moon
So many horrid ghosts.

In another part of the camp we see **Jamy** quietly playing his flute, nearby are **Macmorris, Pistol, Gower, Nym** and the **Boy**. **Fluellen** stands behind this peaceful scene for a moment, before moving on around the camp.

Now, beside a cart, we see the **Chorus**, in the camp. He continues.

CHORUS
O, now, who will behold,
The royal captain of this ruined band

We cut to see **Henry** enter shot in close up and follow him as he makes his way through the camp, meeting with some of his soldiers.

CHORUS
(Voice-over)
Walking from watch to watch, from tent to tent,
Let him cry 'Praise and glory on his head!'
For forth he goes and visits all his host,
Bids them good morrow with a modest smile,
And calls them brothers, friends and countrymen.

Leaving **Henry** to continue, we cut back to close-up on the **Chorus**.

CHORUS
A largess universal, like the sun,
His liberal eye doth give to everyone,
Thawing cold fear, that mean and gentle all,
Behold as may unworthiness define,
A little touch of Harry in the night.

We now cut to **Henry**, standing beside his two worried brothers, **Gloucester** and **Bedford**, as **Erpingham** approaches out of the darkness.

HENRY V
Good morrow, old Sir Thomas Erpingham:
A good soft pillow for that good white head
Were better than a churlish turf of France.

ERPINGHAM
Not so my liege; this lodging likes me better,
Since I may say, 'Now lie I like a king.'

They all smile, glad of some humour on such a night.

HENRY V
Lend me thy cloak, Sir Thomas.

The old knight takes off his cloak, and **Gloucester** helps him put it over **Henry's** shoulders.

HENRY V
Brothers both,
Commend me to the princes in our camp;
Do my good morrow to them; and anon
Desire them all to my pavilion.

GLOUCESTER
We shall, my liege.

The brothers move away. Erpingham lingers a little.

ERPINGHAM
Shall I attend your grace?

HENRY V
No, my good knight;
Go with my brothers to my lords of England;
I and my bosom must debate awhile,
And then I would no other company.

A familiar mask of remoteness has spread across the King's
features. Erpingham can be of no help. He knows as much and
replies compassionately to the young King before leaving.

ERPINGHAM
The Lord in heaven bless thee, noble Harry!

Henry is plainly moved.

HENRY V
God-a-mercy, old heart! thou speak'st cheerfully.

The King moves off to walk around the perimeter of the camp.

English Camp, Another Area: night

The figure of a man rummaging through some bags in the shadows.
It is a familiar one. Pistol looks out from under the awning to check
he isn't being seen before getting back to his thieving. The sound
of a throat being cleared interrupts him and he panics when he
sees a cloaked stranger. Pistol grabs a pike from beside the cart.

The mysterious figure is, of course, Henry, now with the hood of
the cloak up, in disguise. Pistol speaks first.

PISTOL
Qui va là?

HENRY V
A friend.

PISTOL
Discuss unto me; art thou officer?
Or art thou base, common and popular?

HENRY V
I am a gentleman of a company.

PISTOL
Trailest thou the puissant pike?

HENRY V
Even so. What are you?

PISTOL
As good a gentleman as the emperor.

HENRY V
Then you are a better than the king.

Pistol now into his stride but feeling threatened, he unleashes, with full poetic colour, proof of his alleged intimacy with the **King**.

PISTOL
The king's a bawcock, and a heart of gold,
A lad of life, an imp of fame;
Of parents good, of fist most valiant;
I kiss his dirty shoe and from heart-string
I love the lovely bully.

Then, as if to change the subject.

PISTOL
What is thy name?

HENRY V
Harry le Roy.

PISTOL
Le Roy! A Cornish name.

HENRY V
No, I am a Welshman.

PISTOL
Knowest thou Fluellen?

HENRY V
Aye.

PISTOL
Tell him I'll knock his leek about his pate upon
Saint Davy's Day.

HENRY V
Do not you wear your dagger in your cap that day,
lest he knock that about yours.

Pistol starts to back off.

PISTOL
Art thou his friend?

HENRY V
84   And his kinsman, too.

PISTOL
The figo for thee then!

Pistol puts the pike down and prepares to move away from this uncomfortable situation. Henry is amused.

HENRY V
I thank you. God be with you.
PISTOL
My name is Pistol called.
HENRY V
It sorts well with your fierceness.

Pistol scowls and leaves. Henry takes a different direction around the camp.

English Camp, Another Area: night
The ever-zealous Fluellen is checking the camp, urging the men to silence.

GOWER
Captain Fluellen!

Fluellen puts his hand over Gower's mouth to keep him quiet.

FLUELLEN
In the name of Jesu Christ speak lower.

He leads Gower aside to sit down on the shafts of a cart to continue the reprimand.

FLUELLEN
If you would take the pains but to examine
the wars of Pompey the Great, you shall find,
I warrant you, no tiddle taddle nor pibble pabble
in Pompey's camp.
GOWER
Why, the enemy is loud; you hear him all night.
FLUELLEN
If the enemy is an ass and a fool and a prating
coxcomb, is it meet, think you, that we should also,
look you, be an ass and a fool and a prating
coxcomb? In your conscience now?
GOWER
I will speak lower.
FLUELLEN
I pray you and beseech you that you will.

Satisfied that Gower will keep his word, they move off to continue their patrol of the camp.

Henry is touched by the unswerving loyalty of the Welshman. His attention is caught by another group of bedraggled soldiers. He moves off towards them, as we hear the sound of confession being taken.

English Camp, Another Area: night

Michael Williams finishes making his confession and joins two of the other soldiers, **John Bates** and **Alexander Court**, sitting beside a fire, staring out towards the French camp. The cloaked figure of the **King** moving into the background is unseen by the three men.

> COURT
> Brother John Bates, is not that the morning
> which breaks yonder?

He is terrified. There is an air of awful resignation over them all.

> BATES
> I think it be; but we have no great cause to
> desire the approach of day.

> WILLIAMS
> We see yonder the beginning of the day, but
> I think we shall never see the end of it.

Henry shifts his weight, cracking a twig, which alerts the soldiers to his presence. **Williams** swings round, knife in hand, to challenge the stranger.

WILLIAMS
Who goes there?
HENRY V
A friend.

WILLIAMS
Under what captain serve you?
HENRY V
Under Sir Thomas Erpingham.

This seems to satisfy **Williams**, who relaxes, and **Henry** moves towards them to sit down on a log beside **Bates**.

WILLIAMS
A good old commander and a most kind gentleman:
I pray you what thinks he of our estate?
HENRY V
Even as men wrecked upon a sand, that look
to be washed off at the next tide.

Suspicion of this comfortless stranger returns.

WILLIAMS
He hath not told his thought to the king?
HENRY V
No, nor it is not meet that he should.
I think the king is but a man as I am:
the violet smells to him as it doth to me.
His ceremonies laid by, in his nakedness he
appears but a man. Therefore when he sees
reasons of fear, as we do, his fears,
out of doubt, be of the same relish as ours are:
BATES
            (Unimpressed)
He may show what outward courage, he will,
but I believe, as cold a night as 'tis, that
he could wish himself in Thames up to the neck,
and so I would he were, and I by him,
at all adventures so we were quit here.

HENRY V
I think he would not wish himself anywhere
but where he is.

BATES
Then I would he were here alone.

HENRY V
88   Methinks I could not die anywhere so contented

as in the king's company, his cause being just
and his quarrel honourable.

WILLIAMS
      (Under his breath)
That's more than we know.

Bates trying to end this depressing topic.

BATES
Ay, or more than we should seek after;
for we know enough if we are the king's
subjects. If his cause be wrong, our
obedience to the king wipes the crime of
it out of us.

Then Williams, quietly and uneasily, turning on the cloaked figure.

WILLIAMS
But if the cause be not good, the king himself
hath a heavy reckoning to make; when all those
legs and arms and heads chopped off in a
battle, shall join together at the latter day,
and cry all, 'We died at such a place'; some
swearing, some crying for a surgeon, some upon
their wives left poor behind them, some upon
the debts they owe, some upon their children
rawly left. I am afeard there are few die well
that die in a battle; for how can they

charitably dispose of anything when blood is
their argument?
        (Fixing the stranger with a stare)
Now if these men do not die well, it will be
a black matter for the king that led them to it.
HENRY V
        (earnestly, with great passion)
So, if a son that is by his father sent
about merchandise do sinfully miscarry upon
the sea, the imputation of his wickedness, by
your rule, should be imposed upon the father
that sent him.
But this is not so. The king is not bound
to answer the particular endings of his
soldiers, nor the father of his son; for
they purpose not their deaths when they
purpose their services.
Besides there is no king, be his cause never
so spotless, can try it out with all unspotted
soldiers.
He holds the man's gaze for a moment. Then almost to himself

HENRY V
Every subject's duty is the king's;
but every subject's soul's his own.

This last is delivered with such surprising weight of feeling that
even Williams uncomfortably reconsiders his fate.

WILLIAMS
'Tis certain, every man that dies ill,
the ill upon his own head; the king is
not to answer it.

Bates finds new resolve.

BATES
I do not desire he should answer for me;
and yet I determine to fight lustily for him.

The King becomes bolder in his defence.

HENRY V
I myself heard the king say he would not be
ransomed.

This is too much for Williams.

WILLIAMS
Ay, he said so to make us fight cheerfully;

but when our throats are cut, he may be
ransomed, and we ne'er the wiser.

HENRY V
If I live to see it, I'll never trust his word after.

The foolishness of this last statement receives Williams's full
contempt.

WILLIAMS
You pay him, then!

Williams suddenly stands up. Court moves to stand next to him
and Bates grabs the cloaked man as Williams continues.

WILLIAMS
You'll never trust his word after! Come, 'tis
a foolish saying.

Williams tries to tempt the man into a fight over the issue.

HENRY V
Your reproof is something too round: I should be angry with
you if time were convenient.

Williams takes his glove from his belt and in a formal challenge
throws it down at Henry's feet.

WILLIAMS
Let it be a quarrel between us, if you live.

At this moment Bates sees Fluellen and Gower approaching and
intervenes.

BATES
Be friends, you English fools, be friends:
We have French quarrels enough.

The soldiers hurry away, pursued by Gower, as Fluellen cautiously
moves towards the hooded figure. Henry turns to face him and the
Captain realises that it is his King. He does as he is bid, and leaves
the troubled monarch alone.

Henry remains at the fire, removes the hood covering his head and
begins to whisper the painful knowledge. The ever-present ache
of his responsibility.

HENRY V
Upon the king! Let us our lives, our souls,
Our debts, our careful wives,
Our children, and our sins lay on the king!
We must bear all. O hard condition!
Twin-born with greatness, subject to the breath
Of every fool. What infinite heart's ease

Must kings neglect that private men enjoy!
And what have kings that privates have not too,
Save ceremony.
And what art thou, thou idol ceremony?
What drink'st thou oft, instead of homage sweet,
But poison'd flattery? O be sick, great greatness,
And bid thy ceremony give thee cure!
Canst thou when thou command'st the beggar's knee,
Command the health of it?

He takes off the cloak and stands up, moving away from the fire.

HENRY V
No, thou proud dream,
That play'st so subtly with a king's repose;
I am a king that find thee; and I know
'Tis not the balm, the sceptre and the ball,
The sword, the mace, the crown imperial,
The intertissued robe of gold and pearl,
The farced title running 'fore the king,
The throne he sits on, nor the tide of pomp
That beats upon the high shore of this world,
No, not all these, thrice-gorgeous ceremony,
Not all these, laid in bed majestical,
Can sleep so soundly as the wretched slave,

He is standing beside the sleeping figure of one of his men as he
continues.

HENRY V
Who with a body filled and vacant mind
Gets him to rest, crammed with distressful bread;
Never sees horrid night, the child of hell,
But, like a lackey, from the rise to the set
Sweats in the eye of Phoebus, and all night
Sleeps in Elysium; next day after dawn,
Doth rise and help Hyperion to his horse,
And follows so the ever-running year
With profitable labour to his grave:
And, but for ceremony, such a wretch,
Winding up days with toil and nights with sleep,
Had the forehand and vantage of a king.

He is disturbed by the arrival of Erpingham.

ERPINGHAM
My lord, your nobles, jealous of your absence,

Seek through the camp to find you.
HENRY V
Good old knight,
Collect them altogether at my tent;
I'll be before thee.

Erpingham leaves and with him what remains of Henry's
courage.On his knees he tries to banish the invasion of his senses
by fear and the visitation of a familiar ghost.

HENRY V
O God of battles! Steel my soldiers' hearts;
Possess them not with fear; take from them now
The sense of reckoning, if the opposed numbers
Pluck their hearts from them.

The feverish prayer will not work.

Not today, O God!
O not today, think not upon the fault
My father made in compassing the crown!
I Richard's body have interred anew
And on it have bestowed more contrite tears
Than from it issued forced drops of blood.
Five hundred poor I have in yearly pay,
Who twice a day with their wither'd hands hold up
Toward heaven, to pardon blood; and I have built
Two chantries, where the sad and solemn priests
Sing still for Richard's soul. More will I do;
Though all that I can do is nothing worth,
Since that my penitence comes after all,
Imploring pardon.

From another part of the camp.

GLOUCESTER
(Voice-over)
My liege!
HENRY V
My brother Gloucester's voice!
        (now remarkably calm)
I know thy errand, I will go with thee:
The day, my friends, and all things stay for me.

A tear rolls down his cheek, he has done and felt all he can. He
slowly closes his eyes and lowers his head.

French Camp, Hilltop: day

From far below we look to the hilltop near the French camp. The sound of hundreds of horses and their riders approaching. Suddenly we see the advance guard of this great army appear on the brow of the hill. It is the French nobles surveying the scene of the English camp below them. As we cut closer we see at the centre of the group the **Constable, Orleans** and the **Dauphin**. Thunderous noise and excitement.

> CONSTABLE
> Hark, how our steeds for present service neigh!
> DAUPHIN
> Mount them, and make incision in their hides,
> That their hot blood may spin in English eyes.
> CONSTABLE
> Do but behold yon poor and starved band,
> And your fair show shall suck away their souls,
> Leaving them but the shales and husks of men.
> There is not work enough for all our hands.

Montjoy arrives to interrupt this euphoric celebration of their expected victory.

> MONTJOY
> Why do you stay so long, my lords of France?
> Yon island carrions, desperate of their bones,
> Ill-favouredly become the morning field;
> CONSTABLE
> They have said their prayers, and they stay for death.

The time for action has arrived.

CONSTABLE
A very little little let us do,
And all is done. Then let the trumpets sound
The tucket sonance and the note to mount;
For our approach will so much dare the field
That England shall couch down in fear, and yield.

With this last, he turns and leads the French away from the hillside.
The preparations for the ensuing battle swing into progress.

English Lines: day

Meanwhile the English are at their line of defence, a long avenue
of wooden stakes between the battlefield and their camp.
Williams, **Bates** and **Court** are among the soldiers putting the
finishing touches to this barrier, the fierce wooden shafts
sharpened and tilted at a savage angle to the oncoming French
army.

English Camp: day

Inside the camp, **Bedford**, **York** and **Westmoreland** nervously
watch the distant French. **Gloucester** joins them.

GLOUCESTER
Where is the king?
BEDFORD
The king himself is rode to view their battle.

Westmoreland moves away from the younger nobles and joins
Exeter and **Erpingham** to confer a little aside.

WESTMORELAND
Of fighting men they have full threescore thousand.
EXETER
That's five to one; besides, they are all fresh.
ERPINGHAM
'Tis a fearful odds.
WESTMORELAND
        (in deepest frustration)
O that we now had here
But one ten thousand of those men in England
That do no work today!

From behind a tree, some distance away, **Henry** steps out to shout
over the assembled throng of anxious English soldiers to where

the nobles are standing.

HENRY V
What's he that wishes so?
My cousin Westmoreland?

As he continues, he signals for the men to gather round him,
addressing the speech to the whole army.

HENRY V
No, my fair cousin:
If we are marked to die, we are enough
To do our country loss; and if to live,
The fewer men, the greater share of honour.
God's will! I pray thee wish not one man more.
Rather proclaim it, Westmoreland, through my host,
That he which hath no stomach to this fight,
Let him depart:

He begins to move through the camp as he speaks, the men
following him, eager to hear the encouragement.

HENRY V
His passport shall be made,
And crowns for convoy put into his purse.
We would not die in that man's company
That fears his fellowship to die with us.

He pauses momentarily and climbs up onto a cart to continue.
The men still following to listen as the young **King**, no trace of
last night's fear, weaves his spell of honour in tones of quiet,
confident compassion. His strength of feeling undeniable, the
effect bewitching.

HENRY V
This day is called the feast of Crispian.
He that outlives this day, and comes safe home,
Will stand a tip-toe when this day is named,
And rouse him at the name of Crispian.
He that shall see this day, and live old age,
Will yearly on the vigil feast his neighbours,
And say 'Tomorrow is Saint Crispin's.'
Then will he strip his sleeve and show his scars,
And say 'These wounds I had on Crispin's day.'

He is now still, his men gathered around him, as he speaks with
God-given certainty.

HENRY V

Old men forget; yet all shall be forgot,
But he'll remember with advantages
What feats he did that day. Then shall our names,
Familiar in his mouth as household words,
Harry the king, Bedford and Exeter,
Warwick and Talbot, Salisbury and Gloucester,
Be in their flowing cups freshly remembered.
This story shall the good man teach his son;
And Crispin Crispian shall ne'er go by,
From this day to the ending of the world,
But we in it shall be remembered;
We few, we happy few, we band of brothers;
For he today that sheds his blood with me
Shall be my brother; be he ne'er so vile
This day shall gentle his condition:
And gentlemen in England now abed
Shall think themselves accursed they were not here,
And hold their manhoods cheap whiles any speaks,
That fought with us upon Saint Crispin's day.

As a huge cheer goes up from the whole of the army, fired up by
Henry's rousing speech, ready to give their all. **Gloucester** fights
his way through to shout to **Henry**.

GLOUCESTER

My sovereign lord, bestow yourself with speed;
The French are bravely in their battles set,
And will with all expedience march upon us.

HENRY V

All things are ready, if our minds be so.

WESTMORELAND

Perish the man whose mind is backward now!

HENRY V

Thou dost not wish more help from England, coz?

WESTMORELAND

God's will! My liege, would you and I alone,
Without more help, could fight this royal battle!

Henry smiles. Then to his army.

HENRY V

You know your places. God be with you all!

He is interrupted by the ominous arrival of **Montjoy**.

MONTJOY
Once more I come to know of thee, King Harry,
If for thy ransom thou wilt now compound,
Before thy most assured overthrow;

Henry can barely contain his anger.

HENRY V
Who hath sent thee now?
MONTJOY
The Constable of France.
HENRY V
I pray thee, bear my former answer back;
Bid them achieve me and then sell my bones.

Then in an explosion of outrage, the King delivers his opinion
while readying himself for the battle.

HENRY V
Good God! Why should they mock poor fellows thus?
Let me speak proudly; tell the constable
We are but warriors for the working-day;
Our gayness and our gilt are all besmirched
With rainy marching in the painful field;
But by the mass our hearts are in the trim;
Herald save thou thy labour;
Come thou no more for ransom gentle herald;
They shall have none I swear, but these my joints;

A huge cheer goes up from the army.

HENRY V
Which if they have as I shall leave 'em them,
Shall yield them little, tell the constable.

Montjoy is once again convinced and impressed by the King's
strength.

MONTJOY
I shall, King Harry, and so fare thee well:
Thou never shalt hear herald any more.

As Montjoy rides away, Henry returns to his soldiers. York
emerges from the group to kneel before him.

YORK
My lord, most humbly on my knee I beg the
leading of the vaward.
HENRY V
Take it, brave York.

He stands to address the rest of the army one final time before leading them into battle.

> HENRY V
> Now, soldiers, march away;
> And how thou pleasest, God, dispose the day!

At last the time has come to move out to prepare for the start of the fight. **Henry** leads his men as they go down on their knees to cross themselves and kiss the ground upon which they will fight. A final prayer.

English Lines: day

From behind some stakes, the **Chorus** emerges and begins to walk towards us as soldiers run past him towards the battlefield.

> CHORUS
> And so our scene must to the battle fly;
> Where, O for pity! We shall much disgrace
> With four or five most vile and ragged foils,
> Right ill-disposed in brawl ridiculous
> The name of Agincourt.

As he exits, we cut to:

French and English Lines: day

A montage sequence as both sides prepare for the battle. The French nobles, confident of victory with their greater numbers, mount their horses and prepare their weapons. It is the **Constable** who will give the order for the battle to commence and they watch him anxiously for his signal.

On the other side, the worried English nobles try to hide their fear. **Exeter**, **Westmoreland** and **Erpingham** patrol the line of stakes, encouraging the soldiers. **Gloucester** and **Bedford** prepare their horses.

Henry too mounts his beautiful white horse, appearing calm and confident for his men. **Exeter**, now mounted, is handed his mace by **Erpingham**.

The bowmen are lined up and under the watchful eye of **Gower** and **Jamy** prepare their bows for the onslaught.

At last the **Constable** lowers the visor of his helmet and with a great flourish of his arm, signals for the French charge to begin.

We hear the sound of thousands of horses galloping towards the

English. The faces of all the men shown in close-up in their terror
of the horrific noise rushing towards them. **Henry** watches his
men, waiting for the right moment to give his own signal for the
English to move forward and meet the French. The noise of the
charge steadily increases in volume.

The bowmen with their weapons primed, prepare to fire the first

flight of arrows towards the French.

As the sound of galloping hooves grows louder, **Henry** raises his sword in the air, and, as he swirls it above his head, he gives a great yell, and brings the sword down The blood-curdling cry is echoed by many of the men as they rush into battle and we cut to find ourselves in the middle of the filthy, vicious scrum.

Battlefield: day

We are now in the thick of the fighting. The nobles, led by **Henry**, on their horses tightly packed with the French nobles and fighting for their lives.

At the same time the bowmen release their arrows with devastating efficiency. Again and again they fly overhead, each time with the same effect, each time the French losing vast numbers from these deadly weapons. Already the bowmen have the greatest effect, and are beginning to wear down the French who have fewer archers amongst their vast number.

They have instead huge numbers of horsemen. With the mud on the battlefield getting deeper and deeper, vast numbers of the French begin to find themselves bogged down.

But the odds are still very much in France's favour and the fighting is desperate. On the ground the captains and foot soldiers are just as occupied, fighting for their lives.

As the battle continues, we begin to pick out individual incidents from the thick of the fighting. **Pistol** and **Nym** are found crawling through the mud, their concern not to fight the French but to pillage the bodies of the dead soldiers for valuables, as the battle rages round them.

Bates is drowning a French soldier in one of the huge muddy puddles which have built up on the battlefield. **Williams** has taken on a huge Frenchman, but with superior sword work, slits the man's stomach.

Henry is fighting ferociously, surrounded by French horsemen. **York** is in real trouble. The French knights have managed to separate him from the rest of the English and are chasing him away from the thick of the battle. Six men against one. **York** is making desperate attempts to escape. **Henry** and his brothers ride to his assistance but are themselves caught up in more fighting.

Nym, finding another body under some trees, is about to secure another purse, when he is stabbed in the back and slumps over the branches.

Back to the French who are struggling in the scrum. The **Constable** rides away towards another area of fighting. As he crosses a large pool of water, the horse shies as a soldier tries to attack, throwing the **Constable** into the murky pool. The other French princes, now on foot, run into the water to rescue their military leader.

The following action is seen in **Slow Motion**. **York** is now on his feet and cornered. His assailants rush towards him, plunging their knives in as if sticking a pig.

We return once more to the dead face of **Nym** who has been found by **Pistol**. The old man's anguish at the loss of his companion is uncontrollable.

Battlefield, Another Area: day
Now, at normal speed, we see that the wounded **Constable** has been dragged to safety. The **Dauphin**, **Orleans**, **Berri** and **Bretagne** are with him and **Montjoy** watches from his horse.

> CONSTABLE
> Why, all our ranks are broke.

> DAUPHIN
> O perdurable shame!

> CONSTABLE
> Shame and eternal shame, nothing but shame!

With this last desperate cry the **Constable** dies.

> ORLEANS
> Let us die in arms: once more back again;
> We are enough yet living in the field
> To smother up the English in our throngs,
> If any order might be thought upon.
> DAUPHIN
> The devil take order now! I'll to the throng:
> Let life be short, else shame will be too long.

He leads them away to rejoin the battle.

Battlefield, Another Area: day
The body of **York**, draped over the cart where he was killed. **Henry** dismounts and kneels down by his cousin. The rest of the English nobles gather around him. It starts to rain.

> HENRY V
> Well have we done, thrice-valiant countrymen:
> But all's not done; yet keep the French the field.

They return to the battlefield, struggling through the rain as we return to **Slow Motion**.

Battlefield: day
The last stage. We see in close-up **Henry** and the **Dauphin** confront

each other at last and a bitter swordfight ensues. All the other English and French principals are fighting in the same manner. **Westmoreland, Jamy, Bedford, Berri, Orleans, Gloucester, Exeter, Williams,** and many more around them.

We see the **Boy** running, carrying a pennant through the fighting soldiers back towards the camp. He now arrives at the English stakes, glancing back to the battlefield, before running into the camp. A group of French horsemen ride towards him.

On the battlefield, **Henry** has temporarily fought off the **Dauphin** and manages to dispose of another attacker, when alarums are sounded from the direction of the camp. Then the terrified screaming of children.

The other English soldiers have heard the terrifying noises and run towards the camp. **Henry** leaves to follow them.

The first to arrive at the stakes are **Gower** and **Fluellen,** who stop as they see the French raiding party riding away from the camp. They run on towards the devastation.

Henry struggles through the water, the last of the battle still going on around him. He runs as fast as his blood-stained and exhausted body can manage, towards the camp.

English Camp, Boys' Slaughter: day

As **Gower** and **Fluellen** arrive, the scale of the carnage is obvious. Every English boy has been killed. **Fluellen** and **Gower** walk amongst the pitiful pile of corpses as the rest of the English army principals arrive to be greeted by the same dreadful sight.

Fluellen kneels down beside the body of the dead **Boy**, **Gower** is beside him.

> FLUELLEN
> Kill the boys and the luggage! 'Tis
> expressly against the law of arms: 'tis
> as arrant a piece of knavery mark you now as
> can be offered; in your conscience now,
> is it not?
> GOWER
> 'Tis certain there's not a boy left alive.

Fluellen breaks down in tears and, crossing himself, leans his head on the **Boy's** outstretched arm.

The rest of the weary blood-stained army look on, stunned. Finally **Henry** arrives on the bank above them. **Exeter** stands beside him.

In despair he turns his back on the scene to deliver a great howl of rage against the French.

> HENRY V
> I was not angry since I came to France
> Until this instant.

Exeter sees **Montjoy** riding towards them.

> EXETER
> (Voice-over)
> Here comes the herald of the French, my liege.

Henry pulls the herald from his horse, forcing him to his knees. He screams at the unfortunate messenger.

> HENRY V
> How now! What means this, herald?
> Com'st thou again for ransom?
> MONTJOY
> No, great king:
> I come to thee for charitable licence,
> That we may wander o'er this bloody field
> To book our dead, and then to bury them;
> To sort our nobles from our common men;
> For many of our princes – woe the while –
> Lie drowned and soaked in mercenary blood:
> O, give us leave, great king,
> To view the field in safety and dispose
> Of their dead bodies.

This speech has been delivered with a desperate, remote sadness.   109

Henry wants confirmation of what it implies. He is now exhausted and only with great effort can he ask the great question.

>HENRY V
>I tell thee truly, herald,
>I know not if the day be ours or no:

Then quietly and with a sense of its momentousness.

>MONTJOY
>The day is yours.

Henry's strength seems to have ebbed away, as he lowers his head in relief. There is a ghostly hush through which the King speaks.

>HENRY V
>Praised be God, and not our strength, for it.

The King tries to heave himself to his feet, stumbling in the effort, but at last manages to stand, Montjoy behind him, a little apart.

>HENRY V
>What is this castle called that stands hard by?
>MONTJOY
>They call it Agincourt.

Then with extraordinary simplicity.

>HENRY V
>Then call we this the field of Agincourt,
>Fought on the day of Crispin Crispianus.

Montjoy moves away to continue the count of the dead and injured on both sides.

Fluellen quietly approaches the King. He stands silently beside him before speaking.

>FLUELLEN
>Your grandfather of famous memory, an't please
>your Majesty, and your great-uncle Edward the
>Black Prince of Wales, as I have read in the
>chronicles, fought a most brave battle here
>in France.

The exhausted King hears these words as if in a dream.

>HENRY V
>They did, Fluellen.
>FLUELLEN
>Your Majesty says very true: if your Majesty is
>remembered of it, the Welshmen did good service
>in a garden where leeks did grow, wearing leeks
>in their Monmouth caps.

The **King** breaks into an involuntary laugh.

FLUELLEN
Which, your Majesty know, to this hour is an
honourable badge of the service; and I do
believe your Majesty takes no scorn to wear
the leek upon Saint Davy's day.

The power of the Welshman's simple feeling is too much for the
King who speaks the following through tears which he cannot
prevent. He is near collapse.

HENRY V
I wear it for a memorable honour;
For I am Welsh, you know, good countryman.

The **King** breaks down and the two men hug each other.

FLUELLEN
All the water in Wye cannot wash your
Majesty's Welsh blood out of your body,
I can tell you that. God bless it and
preserve it as long as it pleases his
Grace and his Majesty too!

Recovering his composure.

HENRY V
Thanks, good my countryman.

FLUELLEN
By Jesu, I am your Majesty's countryman.
I care not who knows it. I shall confess it
to all the world: I need not be ashamed of
your Majesty, praised be God, so long as
your Majesty is an honest man.

HENRY V
God keep me so.

As **Henry** leads **Fluellen** back into the camp, signalling to **Exeter**
to follow them, we discover a very broken and battered **Pistol**
beside a tree, contemplating his inevitably empty future.

PISTOL
Doth fortune play the huswife with me now?
News have I that my Nell is dead.
Old I do wax, and from my weary limbs
Honour is cudgelled.
Well, bawd I'll turn,
And something lean to cut-purse of quick hand.
To England will I steal and there I'll ... steal.

From this crumpled figure we cut to **Henry** as he sits down with
Exeter, Montjoy and **Fluellen** beside him as the rest of the army
gather around to listen.

HENRY V
Herald, are the dead numbered?
MONTJOY
 (handing him a paper)
Here is the number of the slaughtered
French.

The **King** slowly begins to read.

HENRY V
This note doth tell me of ten thousand French
That in the field lie slain: of princes in this number
One hundred twenty-six: added to these
Of knights, esquires and gallant gentlemen,
Eight thousand and four hundred; of the which,
Five hundred were but yesterday dubbed knights.
Here was a royal fellowship of death.
Where is the number of our English dead?

Exeter provides another paper. As the **King** reads the list, we scan
the faces of the English soldiers as they hear the familiar names.

HENRY V
Edward the Duke of York, the Earl of Suffolk,
Sir Richard Kikely, Davy Gam, esquire.
None else of name and of all other men
But five and twenty.

The English are silent. The miracle rings in their ears.

EXETER
'Tis wonderful!
HENRY V
Come, go we in procession to the village:
And be it death proclaimed through our host
To boast of this or take that praise from God
Which is his only.
FLUELLEN
Is it not lawful, an please your Majesty,
to tell how many is killed?
HENRY V
Ay, captain; but with this acknowledgement,
That God fought for us.

FLUELLEN

Yes, my conscience, he did us great good.

HENRY V

Do we all holy rites:

Let there be sung 'Non Nobis' and 'Te Deum';

The dead with charity enclosed in clay.

And then to Calais; and to England then;

Where ne'er from France arrived more happy men.

As **Henry** stands up, the rest of the army begin to move out into the field beyond, some taking the bodies of the dead boys with them. He walks over to where **Williams** is standing and hands back the glove with which he had challenged him the night before. **Williams** takes the glove gratefully, then suddenly realises that the hooded figure with whom he argued was none other than **Henry** himself. Shaking his head in disbelief, he moves out with the others.

Only a few stragglers remain in the camp, among them is **Court** who we cut to in close-up as he turns his head and starts to sing the 'Non Nobis'.

As we widen out, **Henry** enters the shot carrying the dead **Boy** over his shoulder and we start to move off with him into the devastated battlefield.

Battlefield: day

As the 'Non Nobis' continues, building into a crescendo of voices and orchestra, we remain with **Henry** and the dead **Boy** as he walks slowly and painfully through the carnage and wreckage of the battle, where already men and women are pillaging the bodies of the dead.

Among the vast numbers of weary soldiers and horses who follow him through the field we see the principals of the English army, both dead and alive. He passes **Pistol** holding the dead **Nym**, the **Captains**, the **Nobles** carrying the dead **York**, and **Exeter** trudging slowly through the deep mud.

Henry pauses in his march briefly beside the **Dauphin** and **Orleans** who is cradling the dead **Constable** in his arms, before continuing. As he passes **Montjoy**, French women rush towards him screaming. They recognise him as the man to blame. **Montjoy** holds them back as **Henry** passes and finally moves onto a cart where the bodies of the dead boys are being piled.

He gently lays the **Boy** down, kisses him gently on the head, and then stands up as the rest of the army gather round him as best they can. We cut close on his blood-stained and exhausted face, the dreadful price they have all had to pay for this so-called victory clearly etched into his whole being. His head drops as if in shame.

DISSOLVE TO:

French Palace, State Room: day

To the final bars of the 'Non Nobis'. The French and English nobles gather in the great State Room of the French Palace. The respective royal families line up on either end of a huge table. **Henry** with **Exeter, Westmoreland, Gloucester, Bedford, Erpingham.** The French, wearing mourning bands, are led by the **King** of **France**, with the **Dauphin, Orleans, Montjoy** and **Princess Katherine** and **Alice**, both wearing mourning veils. The **Duke of Burgundy** is with them, until now uninvolved with the dispute over the claim to the throne of France, he is to act as mediator in the negotiations.

The two **Kings** officially greet each other.

> HENRY V
> Peace to this meeting. Unto our brother France
> Health and fair time of day; joy and good wishes
> To out most fair and princely cousin Katherine;
> And, as a branch and member of this royalty,
> By whom this great assembly is contrived,
> We do salute you, Duke of Burgundy;
> And, princes French, and peers, health to you all!
> FRENCH KING
> Right joyous are we to behold your face,
> Most worthy brother England, fairly met:
> So are you, princes English, every one.

116

Both men sit, while **Burgundy** begins his passionate plea for peace.

BURGUNDY
My duty to you both, on equal love,
Great Kings of France and England!
Since that my office hath so far prevailed
That face to face, and royal eye to eye,
You have congreeted, let it not disgrace me
If I demand before this royal view,
Why that the naked, poor and mangled Peace,
Should not in this best garden of the world,
Our fertile France, put up her lovely visage?

As **Burgundy** continues with his speech, we now dissolve through the **King** of **France**'s sad face to the dead **Constable** in **Orleans**'s arms.

BURGUNDY
(Voice-over)
Alas! She hath from France too long been chased
And all her husbandry doth lie on heaps,

Dissolve to **Henry** and then through a montage of all the English dead: **York** being carried by the other nobles, the **Boy, Mistress Quickly, Nym, Bardolph, Scroop,** and finally, **Falstaff.**

BURGUNDY
(Voice-over)
Corrupting in its own fertility.

And as our vineyards, fallows, meads and hedges,
Defective in their natures, grow to wildness,
Even so our houses and ourselves, our children
Have lost, or do not learn for want of time,
Those sciences that should become our country,

Over the next few lines we dissolve to **Henry** and then to a wider shot of the English nobles gathered around their **King**, as they react to **Burgundy**'s words.

BURGUNDY
(Voice-over)
But grow like savages, as soldiers will
That nothing do but meditate on blood,
To swearing and stern looks, diffused attire,

And onto **Burgundy** as he concludes.

BURGUNDY
And everything that seems unnatural.
And my speech entreats
That I may know the let, why gentle Peace
Should not expel these inconveniences,
And bless us with her former qualities.

Henry is immoveable and gently challenging.

HENRY V
If, Duke of Burgundy, you would the peace,
Whose want gives growth to the imperfections
Which you have cited, then you must buy that peace
With full accord to all our just demands.

Caught out as expected, the **French King** goes through the motions of excuse.

FRENCH KING
I have but with a cursitory eye
O'erglanced the articles: pleaseth your grace
To appoint some of your council
To sit with us once more, we will suddenly
Pass our accept and peremptory answer.
HENRY V
Brother, we shall.

As the entire party begin to take their leave, **Henry** continues:

HENRY V
Yet leave our cousin Katherine here with us:
She is our capital demand, comprised

Within the forerank of our articles.

Once again the **King** has no choice. He takes his daughter's hand as if to comfort her.

FRENCH KING
She hath good leave.

The **King** and all the nobles retire from the room to go over the terms of the treaty, leaving a surprisingly nervous **Henry** to get this bit of the deal over with as quickly as possible. **Katherine** sits down at the far end of the table from him, looking away. **Alice** stands beside her, removing both their veils before the conversation begins.

HENRY V
Fair Katherine, and most fair,
Will you vouchsafe to teach a soldier terms
Such as will enter at a lady's ear
And plead his love-suit to her gentle heart?
KATHERINE
Your Majesty shall mock at me;
I cannot speak your England.
HENRY V
       (genuinely crestfallen)
O!
       (recovering slightly)
Fair Katherine, if you will love me soundly
with your French heart, I will be glad to hear
you confess it brokenly with your English tongue.

He is getting nowhere. He may as well start from scratch.

HENRY V
Do you like me Kate?
KATHERINE
Pardonnez-moi, I cannot tell wat is 'like me'.
HENRY V
An angel is like you, Kate, and you are like an angel.
KATHERINE
       (to Alice)
Que dit-il? Que je suis semblable à les anges?
ALICE
Oui, vraiment, sauf votre grace, ainsi dit-il.
KATHERINE
O bon Dieu! Les langues des hommes sont
pleines de tromperies.

HENRY V

       (to Alice, concerned)

What says she, fair one? That the tongues
of men are full of deceits?

ALICE

Oui; dat de tongues of de mans is be full
of deceits; dat is de princess.

Henry understands that she can see right through this formal
courtship.

HENRY V

I' faith, my wooing is fit for thy
understanding. I know no ways to mince
it in love but directly to say, 'I love you':
then if you urge me further to say, 'Do you
in faith?' I wear out my suit. Give me your
answer; i' faith, do: and so clap hands and
a bargain. How say you, lady?

Katherine looks down at the King's outstretched hand. She is
deeply unimpressed by this new 'straightforward' approach.

KATHERINE

Sauf votre honneur, me understand well.

HENRY V

Marry, if you would put me to verses or to dance
for your sake, Kate, why you undid me.
If I could win a lady at leap-frog, or by
vaulting into my saddle with my armour on my
back, I should quickly leap into a wife. I
could lay on like a butcher and sit like a
jackanapes, never off. But, before God, Kate, I
cannot look greenly nor gasp out my eloquence,
nor I have no cunning in protestation.

He now takes her by the hands and turns her to face him. For the
first time she looks at him as he pleads his case.

HENRY V

If thou can'st love a fellow of this temper,
Kate, that never looks in his glass for love of
anything he sees there, let thine eye be thy
cook. I speak to thee plain soldier: if thou
can'st love me for this, take me; if not, to say
to thee that I shall die is true; but for thy
love, by the lord, no;

(reacting to her surprised look)

Yet I love thee too.
If thou would have such a one, take me;
and take me, take a soldier; take a soldier,
take a king.
And what sayest thou then to my love?
Speak, my fair, and fairly, I pray thee.

Katherine looks him straight in the eye.

KATHERINE
Is it possible dat I sould love
de enemy of France?

HENRY V
No, it is not possible you should love
the enemy of France, Kate; but, in loving me,
you should love the friend of France, for I
love France so well that I will not part with
a village of it; I will have it all mine; and
Kate, when France is mine and I am yours, then
yours is France and you are mine.

KATHERINE
I cannot tell wat iz dat.

HENRY V
No, Kate?

He decides to try another approach. Leading her to sit down, he sits on the table facing her, **Alice** standing quietly behind them.

HENRY V
I will tell thee in French, which I am sure
will hang upon my tongue like a new-married
wife about her husband's neck, hardly to be
shook off.
       (he begins his Herculean task)
Je quand sur le possession de France, et quand vous avez le
possession de moi – what then, let me see? Donc votre est
France, et vous êtes mienne.

Katherine cannot control her laughter at the **King's** efforts. **Alice**, too, is having difficulty supressing her giggles.

HENRY V
It is as easy for me to conquer the kingdom
as to speak so much more French, Kate; I shall
never move thee in French, unless it be to laugh
at me.

KATHERINE
(through her laughter)
Sauf votre honneur, le Français que vous
parlez il est meilleur que l'Anglais lequel je parle.
HENRY V
No, faith, is't not, Kate.
But tell me Kate, can'st thou understand
thus much English? Can'st thou love me?

Katherine's laughter has died away.

KATHERINE
I cannot tell.
HENRY V
(in mock exasperation)
Well, can any of your neighbours tell, Kate?
I'll ask them.

He stands up and moves around to stand behind her chair.

HENRY V
By mine honour, in true English, I swear
I love thee: by which honour I dare not
swear thou lovest me. Yet my blood begins
to flatter me that thou dost, notwithstanding
the poor and untempering effect of my visage.
Now beshrew my father's ambition. He was
thinking of civil wars when he got me:
therefore was I created with a stubborn
outside, with an aspect of iron, that when
I come to woo ladies I fright them.

He has now edged around the side of the chair so he can face her.

HENRY V
But, in faith, Kate, the elder I wax the
better I shall appear: my comfort is that
old age, that ill layer-up of beauty, can do
no more spoil upon my face; thou hast me, if
thou hast me at the worst! And thou shalt wear
me, if thou wear me, better and better.

As if she knows what is about to be said, Katherine turns away
from him.

HENRY V
And therefore tell me, most fair Katherine,
will you have me?

Come, your answer in broken music, for thy
voice is music and thy English broken.
Therefore, queen of all, Katherine, wilt
thou have me?

KATHERINE
Dat is as it shall please de roi mon père.

Henry gently turns her head so that she is looking at him.

HENRY V
Nay, it shall please him well Kate: it shall
please him, Kate.

KATHERINE
Den it sall also content me.

HENRY V
Upon that I kiss your hand, and I call you my queen.

As he lifts her hand to kiss it, the quiet intimacy is broken and
the **Princess** leaps up and rushes towards the startled **Alice**.

KATHERINE
Laissez mon seigneur, laissez, laissez!
Ma foi je veux point que vous abaisser
votre grandeur en baisant la main d'une
votre indigne serviteure:
excusez-moi je vous supplie mon très
puissant seigneur.

Henry moves round the chair towards **Katherine**.

HENRY V
Then I will kiss your lips, Kate.

She moves away again as he advances.

KATHERINE
Les dames et demoiselles, pour être baisées
devant leur noces, il n'est pas la coutume
de France.

HENRY V
Madam my interpreter, what says she?

ALICE
Dat it is not be de fashion pour les ladies
of France – I cannot tell what is baiser en
Anglish.

HENRY V
To kiss?

ALICE
Your majesty entendre better que moi.

HENRY V
Ah, it is not a fashion for the maids in
France to kiss before they are married,
would she say?
ALICE
Oui, vraiment.
HENRY V
            (as if suddenly grasping the point)
O Kate!
Nice customs curtsey to great kings. You
and I cannot be confined within the weak
list of a country's fashion: we are the
makers of manners, Kate. Therefore, patiently
and yielding.

They lean towards each other with the throne between them and
kiss.

HENRY V
You have witchcraft in your lips, Kate.
There is more eloquence in a sugar touch
of them than in the tongues of the French
council.

At this moment **Henry** sees the rest of the court return.

HENRY V
Here comes your father.

The young couple hurriedly move away from each other to resume
their places at separate ends of the table as the nobles enter the
room, their negotiations complete.

BURGUNDY
God save your Majesty! My royal cousin,
teach you our princess English?
HENRY V
I would have her learn my fair cousin
how perfectly I love her, and that
is good English.

A murmur of amusement greets this remark and the court takes
up its positions at the table once again.

FRENCH KING
We have consented to all terms of reason.

Henry acknowledges this triumph and the **French King** sadly takes
up the quill to sign the documents in front of him, handing over

the throne of France to this young English king and with it his
daughter as **Henry**'s bride.

HENRY V
And thereupon give me your daughter.

The **French King** joins the hands of the couple, holding them firmly
between his.

FRENCH KING
Take her, fair son, and from her blood raise up
Issue to me; that the contending kingdoms
Of France and England, whose very shores look pale
With envy of each other's happiness,
May cease their hatred, and this dear conjunction
Plant neighbourhood and Christian-like accord
In their sweet bosoms, that never war advance
His bleeding sword 'twixt England and fair France.
HENRY V
Amen.
Now welcome, Kate; and bear me witness all,
That here I kiss her as my sovereign queen.

Once again they kiss and as **Henry** turns to address the court, we
start to move away from them.

HENRY V
God, the best maker of all marriages,
Combine our hearts in one, our realms in one!
As man and wife, being two, are one in love,
So be there 'twixt our kingdoms such a spousal
That never may ill office, or fell jealousy,
Which troubles oft the bed of blessed marriage,
Thrust in between the paction of these kingdoms,
To make divorce of their incorporate league;
That English may as French, French Englishmen,
Receive each other. God speak this. Amen!
ALL
Amen.

The whole court freezes in a kind of tableau. In the foreground,
at the great door, the **Chorus** appears, looking directly into the
camera.

CHORUS
Thus far, with rough and all-unable pen,
Our bending author hath pursued the story,
In little room confining mighty men,

Mangling by starts the full course of their glory.
Small time, but in that small, most greatly lived
This star of England. Fortune made his sword;
By which the world's best garden he achieved,
And of it left his son imperial lord.
Henry the Sixth, in infant bands crowned King
Of France and England, did this king succeed;
Whose state so many had the managing
That they lost France; and made his England bleed;
Which oft our stage hath shown; and, for their sake,
In your fair minds let this acceptance take.

He exits, the doors close on the State Room, and slowly we fade
to black.